ADVANCE PRAISE FOR WORKINGMOMS.CALM

"Each page in *WorkingMoms.Calm* holds the gift of personal truth, showing us just how many wonderful options we have to enrich our own lives and those we most dearly love."

Demi Moore

"A must read for all working families!"

Mark Victor Hansen
Co-creator, #1 New York Times best-selling
series Chicken Soup for the Soul®
Co-author, The One Minute Millionaire

"Danielle Kennedy has written a superb guide to raising children and how to live a joyous and productive life. It should be required reading for all prospective moms, dads, and anyone planning on marriage. And it should remain on their bookshelves. As educators, we recommend it to every working parent in our school."

Jon Maksik, Head Master, The Community School
Leslie Maksik, Director of Elementary School,
The Community School

"*WorkingMoms.Calm* is a redundancy as illustrated with insight and passion by Danielle Kennedy. This book is a must read for all women to deal with a society that considers women super human in terms of their capacity to 'do everything' and sub-human in terms of equal rights. *WorkingMoms.Calm* gives tools we all need for survival. Thanks Danielle."

Laura Day
Author of The Circle and Practical Intuition

"Every mom needs an affirmation for a job well done. Ms. Kennedy's book does just that. This is a book I keep by my bedside table for those times when I need 'a little help from my friends.'"

Denise Simone
Associate Artistic Director, Company of Fools

"I will encourage, no, implore, all the single working mothers and working couples with children who I counsel in my office to read *WorkingMoms.Calm*. Danielle Kennedy enthusiastically offers very wise, responsible, balanced, down to earth directions that can be extremely helpful to all women who want to pursue a successful career and still be good mothers. I was particularly impressed by her vision of a 'family friendly work world' and her emphasis on how husbands can equally participate in a good-parenting plan for two-income families."

James R. Covington
M.Div., M.A., Certified Marriage and Family Therapist
Author of *Confessions of a Single Father*

"Manly men can be moms, too ... and those who are privileged to read *WorkingMoms.Calm* will become even more manly. They'll be inspired to excel at the most important job any parent ever has ... I know; I'm a single 'working mom' and use Kennedy's principles as my life compass. I only wish that every father approached parenting with the practical priority that this book advocates. No mom ... or dad ... will ever regret putting *WorkingMoms.Calm* into practice."

George Walther
"Single Working Mom" to 13-year-old daughter
Author of *Power Talking: What You Say Is What You Get*

"Danielle is a true life story of keeping it all together—business, family, and achieving her goals. This book will help the person who needs to handle different roles in their lives, and keep them all together, for success and happiness."

Tom Hopkins, Chairman, Tom Hopkins International
Debbie Hopkins

"SANENESS and COMMON SENSE is what Danielle Kennedy's *WorkingMoms.Calm* is all about. Excellent ideas with practical and realistic input from a mom of eight who has been there and done that. Nothing escapes her perceptive eye. Give this book to every mom you know!"

Dr. Judith Briles
Author, *Smart Money Moves for Kids—The Complete Parents' Guide* and *The Confidence Factor*

"Danielle Kennedy generously shares with us her hands-on experiences raising a family while pursuing a challenging career. To this she adds the expertise of her many friends and associates, mixes it with a touch of spiritual guidance and comes up with an inspirational look at the clever ways women have learned to cope with the divided loyalties, shortage of time, and feelings of guilt that working mothers inevitably experience. How I wish I had a book like *WorkingMoms.Calm* when I was a young working mom."

Elizabeth Larroquette
Actress

"No one knows how to juggle career and motherhood better than my friend Danielle Kennedy. Her children are living testimony to a motherhood lived following her heart and her brains."

Pamela Sue Martin
Actress, Activist

"This book is so much more than great stories of real women—real mothers who work. It's also about handling all the conflicting demands of life. It's the next best thing to having a group of really good girlfriends who understand, care, and have been there too."

Kate Wright
Organizational Consultant, Life Coach

"I just finished reading *WorkingMoms.Calm*. . . most definitely a 'must-have' for career moms. Having started my real estate career as a young mother of two preschoolers, I felt my way along this path . . . how I wish I could have had this book to guide me. . . . Thanks to Danielle Kennedy, others can do it the smart way and have fun."

Doris Edwards
REALTOR® Sarasota, Florida

"What a find for working mothers—an engaging and practical book that helps put to rest the myth of perfection while still keeping hope alive for any woman who wants to find satisfaction in both her career and her family."

Terry Paulson
Ph.D., Psychologist, Speaker, and
Author of *Can I Have the Keys to the Car?*

"The scope of Danielle Kennedy's book goes far beyond advice for working mothers. It provides guidance for any woman dealing with life's inevitable emotional issues of fear, guilt, anger, and forgiveness. The courage and faith that have guided the author's life and the writing of this book will inspire many women."

Sheri Slater
Mother, Businesswoman, Activist

"Nobody is more qualified to write on the subject of inspiration for working mothers than Danielle Kennedy. She has been a mother to many and an inspiration for all for her entire life. Few can match her wit or engaging way of communicating on the platform and the page."

Patricia Fripp
Author, *Get What You Want*

"Endearing, moving and a must read for all women who struggle to balance career and children, Danielle Kennedy's *WorkingMoms.Calm* has given me a deeper appreciation of the privilege of being a mother in our fast-paced society. The book is a reminder of the importance of using our intuition and, in so doing, honoring both our children and ourselves."

Peg Rometo
Intuitive Healer

"As a 'working mom' myself in the 1970s and 1980s, I can certainly relate and understand the pressures and conflicts. I think there has been a paradigm change in the thinking of young families today—a real treat that Danielle and I never had. We fought for it, battled for it, divorced for it, and lived through it. *WorkingMoms.Calm* will help take families beyond those pressures and conflicts on to a journey of fulfilled living."

Bonnie Benton
Director, Residential Product
Research for The Irvine Company

"*WorkingMoms.Calm* is the resource every working mom needs. No matter what type of career, marital, or economic status you have, this book provides practical advice for being the best mother you can be and achieving success in every aspect of life."

Vicky Bates
Interior Designer

"As a working mom with two young children, I found *WorkingMoms.Calm* to be poignant, and accurately describing of the 'struggles' a mother goes through as she balances time for children, friends, husband, and herself."

Toni Whittington
Head of the Art Department,
The Community School, Sun Valley, Idaho

"Danielle Kennedy practices what she preaches! Since I was a child, I've always been in awe of the way Danny not only looks at life but lives it. She writes from her heart and speaks what she knows. As a mom, I saw Danny love her children as she supported their individual endeavors . . . as a businesswoman I respected her accomplishments. Her book offers the insight we all need to live balanced, healthy, happy lives."

Nicole McGregor
Reporter, KDNX-TV, best friend of Mary Kennedy
(Danielle Kennedy's daughter)

workingmoms.calm

danielle kennedy

THOMSON
SOUTH-WESTERN

Australia · Canada · Mexico · Singapore · Spain · United Kingdom · United States

WorkingMoms.Calm:
How Smart Women Balance Family & Career

Danielle Kennedy

Executive Publisher:
Dave Shaut

Senior Acquisitions Editor:
Scott Person

Developmental Editor:
Allison Abbott

Marketing Manager:
Mark Linton

Production Editor:
Chris Hudson

Manufacturing Coordinator:
Charlene Taylor

Compositor:
Cover to Cover Publishing, Inc.

Printer:
Webcom
Toronto, Ontario

Internal Designer:
Lisa Albonetti

COPYRIGHT
© 2003
by South-Western, a division of Thomson Learning. Thomson Learning™ is a trademark used herein under license.

Printed in Canada
1 2 3 4 5 05 04 03 02

For more information contact South-Western, 5191 Natorp Boulevard, Mason, Ohio 45040.

Or you can visit our Internet site at:
http://www.swcollege.com

ALL RIGHTS RESERVED.
No part of this work covered by the copyright hereon may be reproduced or used in any form or by any means—graphic, electronic, or mechanical, including photocopying, recording, taping, Web distribution or information storage and retrieval systems—without the written permission of the publisher.

For permission to use material from this text or product, contact us by
Tel (800) 730-2214
Fax (800) 730-2215
http://www.thomsonrights.com

Library of Congress Control Number:
200219009

ISBN: 0-324-18750-5

In memory of L. J. J. and E. J. M.

"... with nothing more than
one woman's incredible dream
and her boundless sea of faith."

Daniel Patrick Kennedy

Acknowledgments

Where do I begin? A book like this is never the work of just one individual. Once I knew that I wanted to give a voice to so many courageous working mothers, doors flew open. Starting at the University of Southern California in the 1990s, thank yous to my teacher and mentor Noel Riley Fitch and the important influences of Annie, Gywnn, Jack, Judith Freeman, and the exceptional class of writers who supported me. Thank you to Mark, Scott, and Allison at South-Western who envisioned a brand new future for this book.

Lots of love and appreciation to Demi who so generously gave of her time to write the foreword. But more important for her love, her strong intuition, and deep friendship.

The women in this book who so generously poured their hearts out to me and trusted me to write about their unique journeys.

My husband Mike: thanks for always being my best friend, lover, and confidante. My mother Rose whom I love and honor beyond words. And to my sons and daughters who continue to bestow on me some of life's greatest blessings and toughest lessons.

Contributing Mothers

CATHY MARINO BRADFORD—*married; two children; firefighter and Olympic canoeist and kayaker; resides in California*

GINNA BELL BRAGG—*single; one child; chef for The Chopra Center for Well Being in California*

CANDICE COPELAND BROOKS—*married; two children; founder of Moves, International; author; fitness instructor; workshop and seminar speaker; leading producer of fitness videos*

BETTY J. BROWNER—*single; four children; many grandchildren; lawyer; partner in Browner, Pulido, Sheehan; resides in California*

SHARON M. D'ORSIE—*single; two children; CEO of Eagle Environmental Health, Inc.; resides in Texas*

KATHIE DAVIS—*married; two children; cofounder and vice president of IDEA: The Health & Fitness Source; resides in California*

JANICE FUCHS—*married; two children; vice president and general manager of Rouse Fashion Island Management Company, Newport Beach, California*

SUSAN GAMBA—*married; three children; partner with husband and well-known fashion designer Jimmy Gamba, Jimmy Gamba, Inc.; resides in New York City*

MAREL ANN HANKS, M.D.—*single; one son, one daughter; pediatrics practice in Idaho*

RUTH R. HARKIN—*married; two daughters; attorney; appointed by President Clinton to be president and CEO of OPIC (Overseas Private Investment Corp.) 1993–1997; currently senior vice president for international affairs and government relations at United Technologies*

GAIL HARRINGTON—single; two children; editor in chief of Avenues Magazine

NANCY HAYS—married; three children; CEO of Nancy Hays Entertainment, Inc.; singer/entertainer and producer of industrial shows and ballroom dancing videos; resides in Illinois

KELLY RADAKER JONES, PH.D.— married; two children; President of Radaker Jones & Associates, a consulting firm specializing in constructive organizational change for Fortune 500 companies; resides in California

DANIELLE KENNEDY—married; six children; two stepchildren; two grandchildren; author; actress; lecturer; and CEO of Danielle Kennedy Productions, a sales training and motivational program provider; resides in Idaho

JOANNE KONZ—married; three children; vice president of a mortgage company; resides in Iowa

PAULINE ROSS KYNE—single; three children; choreographer/dancer and owner of The Kyne Dance Academy; resides in California

PATTI MCCORD—married; two children; private consultant; resides in California

PAT MCCORMICK—single; two children and several grandchildren; four-time Olympic gold medalist; founder of Pat's Champs Education Foundation; motivational speaker

VALERIE MENGES—married; one son; owner of Walenta Grinding machinery company and a bridal rental business; resides in Wisconsin

PAT MITCHELL—single; one son; president of Turner Original Productions in Atlanta, Georgia

TOMAZINA MULHEARN—married; two sons, one daughter; four grandsons; co-owner of a multi-office real estate company in California

SHIRLEY PEPYS—married; four children; three grandchildren; entrepreneur and owner of Teddy Bears & Tea Cups, Newport Beach, California

Contributing Mothers   vii

PAULA PERRY—*married; two children; co-owner of Perry's Restaurant; resides in Idaho*

ROSEANNE VITULLO PROTEAU, M.D.—*married; two children; retired pediatrician, specialized in handicapped children*

JUDITH REGAN—*single; two children; president and publisher of the Regan Company; Judith Regan Show, Fox Network*

NAOMI RHODE—*married; three children; many grandchildren; co-owner of SmartPractice, Inc.; motivational speaker and author; resides in Arizona*

KATINA SANDERSON—*one child; Hertz rental car agent; resides in Idaho*

DEBBIE SARNOWSKI —*married; four children; sales executive; resides in Wisconsin*

TERRY SAVAGE—*single; one son; financial expert; author of* New Money Strategies for the 90s; *syndicated financial news columnist; PBS television money expert*

KATHY SMITH—*married; two children; fitness expert and television personality; founder and CEO of Kathy Smith Lifestyles, Inc., in California; major producer of fitness videos*

TRACY TROKE THOMPSON—*single; two children; special assistant in the U.S. Small Business Administration, 1993–1997; currently working for the State of Minnesota*

HEIDA THURLOW—*single; one son, one daughter; CEO of Chantal Cookware, Inc.; resides in Texas*

MARISSA COBB WEAVER—*married; two children; director of the Black Holocaust Museum in Wisconsin*

FLAVIA WEEDN—*two children; writer; illustrator; founder of The Flavia Group; author of forty-five published collections of poetic writings and illustrations including eleven children's books; resides in California*

SARA WILSENSKY—*married; two children; sales manager*

Contents

Foreword xi

Introduction xiii

1. **WAKE-UP CALLS** 1
   The High Price of Perfection 3
   Let Your Conscience Be Your Guide 6
   Are There Good and Bad Guilt Trips? 7
   Holding Ourselves Accountable 10
   Asking for Forgiveness 12
   Forgiveness Is an Attitude, Not a Feeling 15
   Passing Judgment 18
   Answering Dad's Call for Help 22

2. **THE GIFT OF YOUR PRESENCE** 25
   A Family-Friendly Work World 26
   Up Close and Flexible 29
   The Two-Sided Easel 35
   The Work Connection 37
   Road Moms 38
   Some Working Moms Are Dads 41
   Only Temporary 42
   Presence Implies Commitment 43
   Family Goals Make the Balancing Act Worthwhile 45
   Just Say No 46
   Who Needs a Social Life? 48
   The Good Old Mommy Network 50
   Present in Spirit 51

3. **ABOLISHING SLAVERY** 53
   To Honor and Respect One Another 54
   Assert and Train 57
   Grown-Ups with a Clue 59
   New Family Lifestyles 66

Finding and Training the Help 70
The Endless List 74

4. BEING RESPONSIBLE 77
   Your Number-One Priority 80
   The Working Mothers' Exercise Plan
     for Achieving High Energy 82
     How to Begin Your Exercise Program 82
     How to Stick with Exercise 85
     What to Expect When You Start a Program 89
   Healthy Eating Routines 90
   Mental Routines 92
     Kathy Smith's BLT Technique 94
   Family Routines 97
     The Best of Both Worlds Routine 97
     The Ideal-Scene Blueprint/Schedule Routine 99
     The Shifting Gears Routine 101
     The Night-Before Routine 102
     The Saturday Morning Routine 103
     The Airplane Routine 103
     The Car Phone Routine 104
     Avoiding the Last-Minute Panic Routine 104
     The One Calendar Fits All Routine 105
     The Rock-a-Bye Baby Routine 105
     The After-Bedtime Routine 105
     Fifteen Minutes in My Room Routine 106
     The Cook One Day a Month Routine 106
     Thirty Favorite Meals Routine 106
     The Ordering-in Routine 107
     The Eat Out as Much as Possible Routine 107
     Having a Sense of Humor Routine 108

5. MOTHERS ON MONEY: THE NEW RULES 111
   Go Back to School 111
   Quit Trying to Win a Popularity Contest 112
   Forget the All-or-Nothing Rule 112

You May Be Worth Millions 113
New Attitude 115
Hop on the Mommy Track
    That Leads to Nowhere? 117
Mothers Against Being Flat Broke 118
It Doesn't Grow on Trees 125
Living Below Your Means 127
Terry Savage's Financial Strategies for Families 131

6. **TOGETHER WE SHALL OVERCOME 139**
True Grit Mama 140
Never Say Never 143
Graduation Was Their Liberation 148
Mother's Tough Love; A Daughter's
    Incredible Courage 155
Don't Stop the Music 161
All the King's Horses and All the King's Men 165

7. **MAKEOVERS 171**
Beauty and the Beast 172
Ego-Slaying 173
From Human to Divine 180
    People 183
    Crises and Unexplainable Events 184
    Finding Silence 185
Can You Come Out and Play? 192
Inventory of Strengths 194

Notes 199

Foreword

As parents we are always seeking answers, advice, insights, and wisdom to the multitude of challenges and obstacles that we face each day. Whether we are working or stay at home moms, finding and creating balance in our lives seems to be one of our greatest challenges.

Knowing that we are not alone in this sometimes overwhelming struggle is one of the most comforting elements we can discover. It may not be the answer but it is a part of the solution.

Okay, so what is the answer? How do we do it?

As you will find throughout this book, there is no one answer; there are many answers.

With *WorkingMoms.Calm*, Danielle Kennedy has brought together a diverse group of women, who along with Danielle's experience as a working mother of eight, have faced some of the toughest challenges you can imagine. Their stories are familiar; some may even feel as if they are your own.

With courage and honesty each of these women generously share their triumphs as well as their defeats. They bring hope and inspiration through practical lessons of living and learning that turn obstacles into blessed opportunities.

There are few as generous and loving as Danielle Kennedy. Her joy for living is infectious. Her gratitude always present. Each page in *WorkingMoms.Calm* holds the gift of personal truth, showing us just how many wonderful options we have to enrich our own lives and those we most dearly love.

Demi Moore
July 2002

> Every choice we have made in our lives, good or bad, has brought us to this very moment.
> What we seek we already have.
> We just need to remember.
> Then we need to share it.

Introduction

During the last 10 years the lecture circuit has taken me all over the world. My claim to fame is helping companies and individuals improve their productivity. I am honored that industries such as real estate, insurance, tax services, beauty care, health products, etc., continue to take my practical methods of increasing their profits seriously. But the question that keeps popping up in my audiences is "How did you manage to become so successful in business while raising six children?"

Although I have written best-selling books on the subjects of real estate sales and direct commissioned sales in many industries, my dream has been to tackle a book on the challenges I faced juggling family and career life. As I enter the "grandmother era" I can look back with some perspective. I realize now that I and the other mothers in this book were some of the trailblazers for working moms of today. This book contains the wisdom that is only derived when one is willing to admit one's mistakes as well as one's successes. And so from these experiences we share come very specific solutions working parents (Dad should read this too!!!) can apply in their daily lives.

As I wrote this book I thought about the many questions working mothers ask me around the world:

> Is it really possible to be a good mother while maintaining a full-time career?
>
> Was my passion for my work enhancing or hindering our family life?

Why do I feel guilty?

Are the sacrifices required in the long run going to be worth it?

Would my children turn out all right in spite of the breakup of my first marriage?

Do they secretly resent my other life and time away from them?

How do I stack up against other working mothers attempting to balance their lives?

What role does my husband play in this complex lifestyle?

My investigation for the answers to these questions has taken me on a soul-searching journey. This book is the story of that journey.

Out of desperation, the search for answers led me to other working mothers who were on a similar path. This need to know other women like myself and to compare notes with them put me in touch with some of the bravest, smartest, and most honest mothers on the planet: working mothers who opened the doors of their hearts, letting me see their vulnerability, sharing their secrets, lessons learned, and a wisdom only such a journey could instill on a mother's heart and soul.

Make no mistake; I know all mothers are working mothers. What distinguishes the mothers in this book is the full-time job responsibility we have outside the home *in addition* to our vocation on the home front. This was a very rare situation when I entered the workforce in the early seventies. But in the midst of leading my own double life, I looked up one day and noticed I was no longer a social experiment.

Today, more than ever, mothers are doing double duty. More than ever, young women need role models who have painstakingly traveled down this road. The role models in this book come from all walks of life: politics, entertainment, business, and former welfare mothers who emerged to become leaders of their communities.

This book was written straight from my heart. And I know that this is also true of all the other contributing mothers. Because each of us have come from that place of the heart, we are willing to go deep as we reveal our secrets. And so from these places in our hearts we share our individual faith and beliefs. We know that there have been times in our double duty life when only faith has sustained us. By faith we don't necessarily mean religion. We mean a faith in self, perhaps a higher power, a viewpoint that goes beyond human explanation. With that in mind know that this guide is for ALL working mothers—regardless of your belief system. This is not just a survival guide, but a thrive guide. How to really enhance both your family and career. If you apply these lessons, practical solutions, and listen carefully to these inspiring stories, we know that you will have more confidence in your abilities to live and enjoy the bonus world that embraces family and career. Consider myself and every mother in this book part of your circle of supporters.

CHAPTER ONE

Wake-Up Calls

It took a heart-wrenching tragedy to snap me out of my self-absorbed frame of mind. I'll never forget that afternoon in May when my best friend hung herself in her bathroom shower while her husband and two young sons were at Little League practice. At the time, I was a thirty-three-year-old, very ungrateful, single mother of five children, and I frequently enjoyed attending my own pity parties.

My best pal was a gem of a woman: a devoted wife and working mother of two young sons, and she was a fiercely loyal and beautiful friend. A Mary Tyler Moore—the tall, lean, and toothy type. And as my father used to say, "A million-dollar smile and the truest friend you've ever had."

But like so many women who become martyrs without a cause, my friend was trying to keep a stiff upper lip. She was a perfectionist who often felt sad and disappointed in herself. She rarely got a glimpse of what the rest of us so deeply loved and admired about her. Her unawareness of her priceless worth ended up being the reason why her death became the dawning of my resurrection.

My realizations came at lightning speed while I watched the four paramedics press a fibrillator on her chest and stick needles around her heart during the ninety-mile-an-hour ambulance ride to the emergency room. Twenty years later, waves of sadness still overwhelm me at the sound of a siren.

How can I ever forget what I came home to after leaving the hospital? All eyes were fixed on me. My five children and my friend's two sons were all sitting together, motionless, on the couch, almost looking like frozen, stiff, uncut paper dolls. No stereos blasting, no pillow fights, no one gaping in the refrigerator. It was the saddest sight you could ever imagine.

Nobody is perfect, so stop picking on yourself.

I bent down on my knees in front of her boys, unable to look either one of them in the eye. It took every ounce of strength I could muster to whisper, "She's gone."

It was at that precise moment when I snapped, as I held her sons in my arms, each of us sobbing and shaking so hard I thought our hearts would explode and splatter all over the room. It was as if some invisible force was shaking loose my old, ungrateful self.

Up until her death, there was always something I could bitch about or another reason to feel sorry for myself. I was constantly slipping back into the past, feeling guilty about my divorce, even my successful career. It had been a long time since I lived in the present moment.

In the months following her death, I came to a silent resolution: Never again would I expect perfection of myself. I vowed to do the best I could with the time allotted and then put the rest of my worries and cares behind me or into the hands of my maker.

I resolved to never again take life—each breath, each moment—for granted. I not only vowed to live this way for the sake of myself and my family but out of respect for the memory of my dearest friend. I believed my renewed gusto and exuberance for life would be a way to breathe her spirit back into existence. We shared so many of the same dreams. By living mine, I've since felt I am taking her along with me in spirit. I often make a secret toast to her when I celebrate one of my new blessings.

Sometimes, very early in the morning, I stand on my deck and face the mountains. Silently, I say to the breeze blowing around me, "Are you there, my friend? Please come and enjoy this day with me."

As I write this book, I believe she is close at hand; I hope she understands that her life was not lived in vain.

THE HIGH PRICE OF PERFECTION

Chantal Cookware's Heida Thurlow got her wake-up call during her bout with cancer and chemotherapy treatment.

"When I grew up, my parents practiced the philosophy: Work to live. Our family always took two or three vacations a year. My parents played as hard as they worked.

"In my pre-cancer days, I forgot everything they taught us. I worked like a maniac at the office. Then, without missing a beat, I'd go home and push myself and the children even harder. The moment cancer hit, it was like an eye-opener. Heida, are you crazy? Is this what life should be all about?"

Be aware of the dangers of perfectionism.

During Heida's chemotherapy treatments, she made arrangements to buy a mountain home in Park City, Utah.

"It was my dream to go there and ski with my children. While growing up in Germany, my parents always took us to the mountains. Suddenly, it seemed so important to have that kind of fun again."

Heida Thurlow knows firsthand, having survived cancer, that having fun is one way of loving yourself.

"For some reason, we get selfishness mixed up with loving ourselves. No one can raise good children or be successful on the job long term without learning to do this."

Now that Heida has mastered the art of taking care of herself, she enjoys teaching other women how to do it, too. She spends her extra time at The Women's Center in

Houston, Texas, where she teaches job readiness to women who are about to make some important changes in their lives.

"It is a shelter for homeless and abused women. Our success rate is phenomenal because we do things differently, and it works. For example, the shelter is small—only thirty-seven women. And it is a long-term home—not a place a woman comes for a month to get fixed. They stay at least one year.

"It is very comprehensive. It includes psychotherapy treatment. Then the women take classes in job readiness and how to function in the work world. Some enter the shelter uneducated or they haven't worked for a long time. Other women had careers but became addicted to drugs. They are afraid to get back into the workforce. No matter what their age, educational level, or experiences are, they all have one thing in common: no self-esteem."

I asked Heida if the children live with their mothers during the healing process.

"Absolutely not," says Heida. "'Our philosophy is: Heal yourself first before you try to take care of your children.

"Think of it this way: When you are on an airplane, the stewardess instructs parents, in case of an emergency, put their own oxygen masks on first."

My own personal history, in combination with my research for this book, confirms the shelter's philosophy. Most of us women do not need to be told how to take better care of our families or our careers. Entrepreneur Shirley Pepys says her company was fast becoming a runaway success and her family was thriving when she hit the skids. "Everybody concerned got a big chunk of my time and energy except yours truly," says Shirley.

"I see young mothers in my company ready to explode. They panic if they aren't home at exactly six o'clock and the dinner isn't three-course gourmet. I ask them if their husbands cook. Of course not, and no way is he going to put food on the table."

"I was one of those young mothers who once believed I must do everything. Then I got very resentful, and those feelings turned to guilt. And then the guilt turned into shame, which led to my long depression. I was so exhausted and so sure I was dying of something. I had bad headaches, too, which made me think of brain tumors. I spent thousands of dollars getting tests run. MRIs, you name it."

Allow guilt, not shame, to guide you to doing the right thing.

Shirley says the scariest part of her depression was the sad feelings that invaded her spirits.

"I felt so hopeless and exhausted. That hopelessness is what I am on a mission to stamp out with young women."

Several years of therapy, along with making major lifestyle changes, has placed Shirley on her own highway to happiness. Her counselor couldn't believe that a woman who started a baby blanket business out of her garage, turning it into a thirty-million-dollar operation, was such a wimp.

"I never gave myself any slack. I've come out of this very lucky. My diagnosis could have been fatal."

Women are clever chameleons. Petite and perky financial wizard Terry Savage had everybody fooled, including herself.

"I got my wake-up call when my kidney stopped functioning and I was rushed to the hospital in the midst of trying to be all things to all people.

"You know the routine: In charge of the biggest fundraising event in Chicago. Writing a money show for kids for public television. Editing and performing my own segment on the twice-nightly news. Delivering cookies to the school for my son's party. Back to the studio to do the news. Then back to the school on time to watch my son perform in his Christmas concert."

Terry kept running on empty until her brain gave her the message: "You are out of fuel, girl."

"I was feeling really lousy. Taking lots of aspirin every morning thinking it was just the flu. When you have this kind of responsibility, you just tell yourself you are not allowed to get sick."

Ultimately, she was rushed to the hospital. After ten days of tests, it was discovered her kidneys had shut down and she needed surgery to reset her urethra.

"My double life came to a screeching halt. All I could do was lay on the flat of my back and think. I'd watch the stock market news on television. It rose to a new high. I watched my money show continue successfully with the help of a fill-in. And then some realizations dawned on me:

"One—I am not indispensable. Life does go on with or without me. The news anchor who replaced me was doing just fine. I lightened up quite a bit. Can any of us take what we do quite that seriously?"

> **You are morally obligated to take care of yourself.**

Terry said so-called super-moms tend to think we *have* to do this or that. In the last chapter, you will learn that this message comes from your ego.

"I crammed more stuff into one day. It was as if I was shouting to everyone, 'Look at perfect little Terry.' Then, suddenly, I find myself flat on my back for one month. Off work for another five weeks. The sad part was, nobody really gave a hoot.

"Two—When my kidneys shut down, I thought I might die. I was forty years old. Up until then, I thought I was invincible and could do anything. Suddenly, I knew what a gift good *health* was. None of us have the right to neglect taking care of ourselves."

LET YOUR CONSCIENCE BE YOUR GUIDE

So how *does* a working mother strike a balance in her multifaceted, demanding life? How do we know when to draw the line? After my friend's death, I became much more aware of the long-term consequences of making daily, responsible decisions that not only enrich my family and career but also myself.

My conscience became my best monitor for determining appropriate behavior while juggling. A developed conscience uses feelings of guilt as a red flag. Those feelings become our wake-up call to guide us as we prioritize and discern what would be the most moral thing to do.

Activate your conscience.

Without a conscience, we could not distinguish between right or wrong. There are so many choices put on our paths. Our hearts are often distracted by our beastly egos (see Chapter 7). A further complication is all the unsolicited advice working mothers get regarding the "right" thing to do. Combine our egos with all the unsolicited advice and you end up with a bunch of insecure, confused women. The trick is to learn how to distinguish between the guilt that is self-imposed and the guilt that is triggered by a healthy conscience.

ARE THERE GOOD AND BAD GUILT TRIPS?

Guilt feelings run strong when we must leave our children for part of every day to earn a living. Some of our guilt is self-imposed and unnecessary. I've noticed over the years that there is a big difference between the way mothers and fathers say good-bye to their families as they go off to work or even a social event.

Usually, when Dad leaves for work or fun, he just says, "Bye, gang, I'm going to work now," or "See you later, I'm going to play golf with the boys," as he nonchalantly dismisses himself.

Mom, on the other hand, often sneaks out the door like a criminal, while the baby-sitter attempts to distract the child with food or games.

Joanne Konz tries to keep her coming and going in perspective: "When my daughter was two, she got hysterical when I left for work. She'd be hanging on me as I dragged myself out the door. This may sound cold, but I know when a child is two and a half that is just how a two-year-old acts. Period. It's a phase. Plus I always call my sitter when I get to work and ask her how long my daughter was hysterical. 'About two minutes,' she tells me, as I hear my daughter giggling in the background."

Once Joanne realized it was just a phase, she began handling all morning good-byes with "an extra hug at the door. Then I told her I must leave to go to work, but I would be back at a certain hour. I always come back at that time, so she eventually trusted me and grew out of the phase."

All parents should feel a certain amount of guilt at the appropriate times as a signal to monitor both their own actions and their children's behavior. An active conscience produces guilt feelings for good reason.

For example, if Joanne kept promising her daughter that she would be home at a certain time but was usually a few hours tardy, wouldn't her conscience have good reason for imposing some guilt?

My friend's suicide taught me that there was a big difference between normal guilt feelings and runaway shame. Guilt only serves a good purpose if it leads to a higher moral awareness. Such an awareness triggers more appropriate behavior such as coming home on time. Good guilt enables us to self-correct and change our misbegotten ways that are often the result of poor judgment, emotional immaturity, and selfishness.

A study of over 1,100 babies in nine states, enlisting the aid of twenty-five researchers, released a preliminary joint report on the effect of day care on babies' attachment to their mothers.

One conclusion of the study brings home loud and clear the need to continually use our conscience to make proper moral decisions in the area of work and family.

Jay Belsky, a professor of human development who has spent most of his professional life researching both working and stay-at-home moms, is one of the twenty-five researchers.

He says, "The more cavalier mothers were about day care for babies, the more likely their kids were to be insecure. Being concerned or anxious about work served your baby well."

And he added, "I grew up in a Jewish family. Guilt is not so bad. A reasonable amount of worry is well spent."

Personally, it took a while for me to learn how to distinguish between what I should feel guilty about and what was merely an embarrassing reaction to not doing the popular thing. For example, take my decision to become a working mother. I stayed home the first seven years of my motherhood with no intention of going out into the world to find more work. With four children under seven at home, I had all the work I needed in my own backyard.

But when my husband's pay went from a thousand dollars a month to four hundred dollars, I had no choice. Remember, it was the sixties. Back then, a working mother was like a social experiment. And I was a pregnant one (expecting number five), which made me even more unusual.

Most of the moms in my neighborhood were still home all day. Looking back, I think I felt more guilty about not following the crowd than about working. It seems to depend on the era of time we are mothers and what the norm is. Ironically, today's stay-at-home mothers tell me they feel guilty because in their neighborhoods, a majority of their peers are now in the workplace.

Nobody should take time to feel guilty unless their behavior is inappropriate. For example, leaving children in day care for long periods of time with no qualms about working long hours, playing golf all day, or excessively volunteering for charitable causes is a reason to feel guilty. And both parents, not just the working mother, should be held accountable and be prepared to make necessary changes in the routine.

Be accountable.

In reality, those of us who are responsible working parents have much to offer our children. We are a team, taking turns nurturing them as we simultaneously develop our individual talents. All this growth takes place as we each improve our family's financial status. What could be a healthier environment for growing a family?

When parents share the responsibility, without the excessive use of outside babysitters or nannies, a child grows emotionally strong and mature and receives the added benefit of living with two very interesting individuals.

Holding Ourselves Accountable

Two of this book's greatest role models who have a thirty-year history of a happy marriage, outstanding adult children, and highly successful careers are Jim and Naomi Rhode. From the beginning of their marriage, Naomi and Jim began implementing habits and establishing priorities to ensure the success of their family life.

One of the ways Naomi has been able to make good choices both at home and at work: "My Accountability Group. There are six of us women who have met for over ten years for six hours each month. Two- to three-hour sessions at a time. We are all professional, Christian women with families, and our purpose is to hold each other accountable."

They ask each other questions such as:

Are you working too hard?

How healthy are you right now?

Have you had enough time alone with your spouse?

Individual children?

Yourself?

God?

Naomi feels, "If my family is emotionally healthy, then I find I am a much better professional. It is a synergistic energy. When we neglect family, we neglect our careers and vice versa."

I am part of a women's accountability group, too. We call ourselves the RENEW group because our goal is to keep renewing ourselves. Growth is our goal. Spiritual, mental, physical, family, work, financial. We each know that if any one of us is in trouble we can count on each other for comfort and assistance. Children's accidents, births, deaths, all the joys and sorrows of our existence, we share with each other. We tell each other problems that we wouldn't feel comfortable sharing with anyone else. And because the trust exists between us, we are willing to be accountable to one another. The advice we give one another is always done with gentleness and love.

You too can form an accountability group. It can be informal. It works when you all share similar personal beliefs. For instance, if you struggle with working late, then enlist a friend or an accountability partner who can help you get a perspective on being obsessive. This method can work for any situation or issue—work, diet, money, time—just as long as you are honest with the other person. Usually just stating your concern out loud to another person is enough to warrant change. Knowing that this person will keep you accountable to change is enough motivation for most people. Personally, I've noticed as I have gotten older that I really am so grateful for my close girlfriends in my RENEW group. There is a trust, understanding, and a history between us that even spouses and children cannot replace.

Asking for Forgiveness

Naomi believes one of the most important ways we hold ourselves accountable is to stay reconciled with each other through many acts of forgiveness.

"Reconciliation not only brings peace but helps us renew our perspective. When I started speaking and traveling, my children were in their late high school and early college years. But I felt my youngest daughter Katherine was cheated the most because I traveled when she was a young teenager.

"So when she was in college, I took her to high tea one afternoon, something I still often do with my daughters. I apologized to her and told her that I really felt like I had cheated her. I started to cry, and I asked her to forgive me if I was gone too much when she was in high school.

Ask forgiveness of your children and others.

"She became furious with me, saying, 'The privilege of being raised in this home was so awesome. The travel that your work afforded for us. The multiplicity of experiences. The understanding we have about life and people so far surpasses any little inconveniences that I might have experienced in your short absences. I don't ever want to hear you say that again.'"

Naomi's story made me cry. I related to her enormous sense of relief her daughter's comments gave her. My story, entitled "Lesson from a Son," which I wrote for Jack Canfield and Mark Victor Hansen's *Chicken Soup for the Soul*, has a similar lesson about taking the opportunity to ask for forgiveness.

Lesson from a Son

My son Daniel's passion for surfing began at the age of thirteen. Before and after school each day, he donned his wet suit, paddled out beyond the surf line, and waited to be challenged by his three- to six-foot companions. Daniel's love of the ride was tested one fateful afternoon.

"Your son's been in an accident," the lifeguard reported over the phone to my husband Mike while I was out of town on business.

"How bad?"

"Bad. When he surfaced to the top of the water, the point of the board was headed toward his eye."

Mike rushed him to the emergency room and they were sent to a plastic surgeon's office. Daniel received twenty-six stitches from the corner of his eye to the bridge of his nose.

I was on an airplane, flying home from a speaking engagement while Dan's eye was being stitched. Mike drove directly to the airport after they left the doctor's office. He greeted me at the gate and told me Daniel was waiting in the car.

"Daniel?" I questioned. I remember thinking the waves must have been lousy that day.

"He's been in an accident, but he's going to be fine."

A traveling working mother's nightmare had just come true. I ran to the car so fast the heel of my shoe broke off. I swung open the car door, and my youngest son with the patched eye was leaning forward with both arms stretched out toward me and crying, "Oh, Ma, I'm so glad you're home."

I sobbed in his arms, telling him how awful I felt about not being there when the lifeguard called.

"It's okay, Mom," he comforted me. "You don't know how to surf, anyway."

"What?" I asked, confused by his logic.

"I'll be fine. The doctor says I can go back in the water in eight days."

Was he out of his mind? I wanted to tell him he wasn't allowed to go near the water again until he was thirty-five, but instead, I bit my tongue and prayed he would forget about surfing forevermore.

For the next seven days, he kept pressing me to let him go back on the board. One day, after I emphatically repeated "No" for the hundredth time, he beat me at my own game.

"Mom, you taught us to never give up what we love."

Then he handed me a bribe—a framed poem by Langston Hughes that he bought because "It reminded me of you."

It was the poem, "Mother to Son."

Since I wrote that story, I have received dozens of letters from other guilt-ridden mothers who thanked me for being so honest about my feelings. The real lesson of that story is that my son never even thought to charge me as guilty for being absent at the time of his accident. I charged myself as guilty. So do other working moms.

Sometimes our feelings of guilt should signal us to take positive action, such as **forgiving oneself and asking others for forgiveness**. Harboring unnecessary guilt is a negative action that usually manifests itself through spontaneous outbursts of anger and resentment.

Take the case of a bitter single mother, someone who I once was. If you are that person right now, I can honestly sympathize when you tell me you and your children have lived through a painful divorce. But you can make a decision right this second to **stop dwelling on the experience**. Instead, change how you think about what happened to you. Look at it this way:

When you experience pain and loss, your consciousness has been stretched. In the long run, your newly stretched consciousness will transform you into a much more caring and compassionate human being than you were before the crisis.

Resurrection always follows a death. However, if you choose to harbor unnecessary guilt, which continues to make you angry and bitter, you cut off your chances of experiencing a series of glorious resurrections.

FORGIVENESS IS AN ATTITUDE, NOT A FEELING

The secret is to grant your enemies, including your ex-husband, forgiveness. Think of forgiveness as an attitude. It is *not a feeling*. It's a decision. This attitude does not require you to seek this person out and personally tell him you are sorry or to expect him to do likewise.

It means in the depths of your heart you say to yourself, "I will not hold it against you. I cannot say I forgot what happened because the event [death or divorce] does not change. But the way I can relate to that event has the power to transform me."

I felt guilty when my first marriage, which produced five wonderful children, ended after fourteen years. But I made the decision to confront my guilt head-on by apologizing to my children for the pain their father and I caused them. Our children deserved our deepest, most heartfelt expressions of pardon. They never asked to be born, much less to be born into a broken home.

After they each willingly accepted my apology, I told them the story of the birth and death of their parents' love. I didn't try to hide our faults and failures, because it was important that they knew they were not responsible for

> If you are a single mother, do an autopsy on your marriage's death.

the breakup. Their father and I, not them, made this unfortunate situation happen.

I literally conducted an autopsy to explain what I best understood to be the cause of death—a lack of unconditional love on both of our parts. I concluded the explanation with, "Learn from your parents' mistake. But most of all, I hope this makes you more compassionate toward everyone."

Some time after our forgiveness session, one of my sons wrote the following:

> *My father and mother are both very brilliant individuals who came to a point in their lives where they were no longer two oxen working in unison to pull the same cart. I believe that they were people lacking faith in each other, and they were controlled by fearful minds that offered no guidance.*
>
> *The most awful part about the divorce is that for roughly ten years, I let someone else's mentality harm me because I was fearful, uncertain, and lacking faith in myself. I was the direct product of their failing relationship, but only because I made it that way. I have since learned to forgive, and in doing so, I have come to understand the fruition that true love and faith can offer. Now my heart seems to speak to me through a free-flowing, creative medium that is prevalent in all aspects of my life.*

My daughter wrote of her hard-won wisdom:

> *I am the child of divorce. I witnessed battle at an early age. I was also the recipient of much love. I don't feel obligated to say that. I was. Love and fear can live in perfect harmony, oddly enough. But people don't slow down on an open road to watch two people holding hands. You can be sure, however, that they'll hit the brakes like a game-show buzzer to see wreckage and pain and human suffering. We see this stuff and we don't forget. But we can forgive, and in the process of forgiving, we heal.*

Forgiving doesn't necessarily mean forgetting. My children and I will always remember that sad time in our lives. I am glad I felt deep sadness and guilt, and I know it is a part of divorce's territory. Too many adults today try to make light of it. "Oh, the kids are better off without their Mom or Dad."

Divorced parents have no idea how badly their children want them to become civil to each other again. Granted, in some cases, there is never that possibility, but when even a tiny door of opportunity to forgive opens, don't be afraid to walk through it.

A few years back, this lesson was clearly brought home to me. It was on the occasion of my second youngest daughter's college graduation. Along with my husband Mike and our whole family, my ex-spouse, his wife, and their son Patrick also attended.

Unbeknownst to me, at one point during the graduation ceremony, two-year-old Patrick walked over to our ten-year-old daughter Kathleen, who promptly lifted him up on her lap. Grama told me later that when my oldest daughter saw Kathleen do that, she started to cry.

My daughter told my mother later that day, "It took the children from their new families to help heal our old one."

Before you read any further, take the time to either write or call your children and let them know how very sorry you are for all the pain they have endured because of your mistakes. Many single mothers tell me that this process initiated all their future healings.

Us winning working moms successfully learn how to balance our lives by listening for new wake-up calls that can take us to a higher spiritual level. When opportunities present themselves to diffuse anger, guilt, and rage by forgiving, we jump at the chance to respond. Our juggling act requires that we have plenty of energy. And we know that negative emotions have the power to drain us of our strength.

Passing Judgment

Criticizing each other is another hurtful pastime and energy drainer, so let's initiate a few more wake-up calls with the purpose of healing past wounds. Don't all mothers work their tushes off? Isn't it time to wake up and stop passing judgment on each other?

Never pass judgment on other families.

Patti McCord's husband is a pastor and she's felt such righteous criticism. "I get judged subtly. Whether it is a neighbor or one of my husband's parishioners saying, 'I could never do that.' It is not like I have decided to leave my kids. When a mother has to work, you want other mothers in the community you work in to support you. Not by raising your kids but through their emotional support."

Bottom line, what distinguishes working mothers is our breadwinner status. Couldn't any family's financial situation change at the drop of a hat? So who has the right to pass judgment?

When I was a single mom selling real estate and fantasizing about princes on white horses appearing at my door, I got a call from one of those lucky stay-at-home moms. She was the wife of a successful doctor. They were married thirty years, and all four of their daughters were now married.

I'll never forget what this "lucky" woman said to me the day I went over to her house and put it up for sale: "I can't believe my husband wants a divorce. I thought we had the perfect marriage. He's left me in a terrible bind. I have no job skills. I've never even balanced our checkbook. Now I have to sell this beautiful mansion and move into some dump condominium. You are so lucky you can support yourself and your children, Danielle."

She snapped me out of my "if I had a rich man" fantasy real fast. Suddenly, I didn't want to trade places with her for all the Prince Charmings of the world. None of us know when circumstances will change our status from stay-at-home mother to a working mother. So everybody needs to bite his or her tongues.

During the few years I did not work outside of the home, I did earn money addressing envelopes and baby-sitting for my next-door neighbor's newborn. She was a dental hygienist with a thriving practice.

I was more than happy to watch her baby. I had a newborn myself, so I figured, what's another bottle in the warmer? Plus we needed money very badly. I will always be grateful for that time in my life when a stay-at-home mom and a working mother joined forces to help each other out.

Eventually, I went to work full-time myself because I couldn't justify our low standard of living. It was doing nobody any good, including myself. I saw the talents of my family blossoming, and I wasn't going to just stand by and do nothing about it. Dancing lessons, guitar lessons, and Little League uniforms all cost money.

I had a guilty conscience about being broke, knowing full well I had talents that could end this financial misery.

Who really has the right to pass judgment on a woman's decision to stay home or go to work? One lady who did pass judgment on all mothers who work outside of the home got her wake-up call, but not until she herself became a mother. "I was one of those kids who was raised by a working mother. When I got married and started my career, I was very arrogant. I always criticized my neighbors who had children and went off to work every day.

"When we got married, my husband and I decided that we would both work for five years and then we would have a baby. Once the baby came, I'd take myself out of the job market. None of that working mother stuff for me. I would never do to my child what my mother did to me.

"Six months after my baby was born, I was climbing the walls. I loved my baby more than life, but I couldn't see myself just taking care of her all day, not to mention the financial pinch we were feeling as a family now that my income was nonexistent. I couldn't help thinking that I could be doing more to help my husband with our financial situation. And I truly knew it would not take away from me being a good mother."

This whole experience helped her reevaluate her relationship with her own mother, who she realized she had been terribly hard on. "I appreciate and love her now in a way I should have much sooner in life. I know now what a great job Mom did in spite of my ungrateful attitude."

She ultimately decided to go back to work on her terms. She became a home-based entrepreneur. Today, she is in the top 1 percent of sales in the nutrition industry, and her four-year-old daughter is "an absolute joy."

So, is the moral of the story to go back to work after you have a baby? Or does the answer have more to do with being painfully honest with yourself regarding what works for you and your family and what doesn't work?

That is what one Wall Street whiz who wishes to remain anonymous discovered.

"I was one of those fireballs who wasn't going to let a baby stop me from becoming number one in my firm. Two weeks before I left on maternity leave, I told my department manager that I would be back when the baby was four weeks old."

She and her husband interviewed au pairs and hired one who was both nurse and nanny.

"I thought this whole baby thing was a walk in the park, and I could handle anything."

Then her daughter Tiffany was born.

"I turned into a blithering idiot. I couldn't keep my hands or eyes off the child. I was just like Shirley MacLaine from that scene in *Terms of Endearment*, crawling in to Tiffany's room at all hours of the night to see if she was still breathing."

There was no way she could go back to work when her baby was four weeks old—or four months, for that matter.

Her husband had to quit his job and find one that paid more money.

"Tiffany is now a year old. I wouldn't have missed this time of my life for any multimillion-dollar deal on Wall Street. I'll probably go back to work in a few more years."

There is yet a third story with a different mother's twist. This stay-at-home mom was raised as the daughter of a very successful businesswoman of the 1950s who ran a multimillion-dollar cosmetics company.

"My mother had no choice. It was a given she would take over the company her father had named after her before she was even born. She was his darling and the one who would follow in his entrepreneurial footsteps."

By the time her mom was nineteen, she was representing the company internationally and traveling all over the world. When she married and had children, nannies and aunts were hired and put in charge.

"Mom hated the travel after she had us, but she always was expected to march to her father's music. She left frequently, and I would throw up for hours after she left on a business trip."

It took years of therapy for this woman to get over her mother's absence while she was growing up.

"I vowed to never work while my kids were growing up. I just felt it was my responsibility to be there. But many of my women friends work. I don't judge them. I can see they are very different than I am. I am sure that has something to do with our different backgrounds.

"I cannot believe what some of these working moms take on. I am not built that way emotionally. I know for me it is important not to take on more than I can handle because if I do, I fall apart. I had one nervous breakdown already when my children were little."

This story from a stay-at-home mom comes from the daughter of a working mom who did not draw the line. And so her daughter grew up with a whole different perspective than I did or someone like Ruth Harkin, who has never found a need to justify to her children why she had to leave them and go to work.

"Guilt is not a part of my history. I am from a long line of working mothers, all who had common sense. They just followed their hearts back and forth between home and business. And we are a pretty normal, happy bunch.

"My maternal grandmother ran a restaurant in Saint Paul, Minnesota, during the depression. A café. Later, she became a domestic. My experience of going to visit Granny? Going to work with her when she cleaned houses. This was exciting and wonderful to me. I wanted to grow up and be just like her."

Ruth always knew she would work and have a family. "There was never an either/or choice here. When people decide they want a career and family, they must understand they are giving up some control.

"Instead of distracting myself with guilt, I stay focused—a difficult challenge in the beginning of new motherhood but easily accomplished with plenty of practice.

"If there is a conflict between work and home, I see what I can work out. When, given two choices, I ask myself, 'What is really important here? Do I really care if the rug is vacuumed three times a week? Is it important that I am there to witness the vacuuming?'"

Working mom and pediatrician Dr. Marel Hanks advises, "Young mothers best consult their hearts in regards to the early nurturing of their babies. The heart knows the answer. For some mothers, staying home twenty-four hours a day is not the answer."

Answering Dad's Call for Help

What about the working dad who is beginning to listen to his own heart? Perhaps he hates his job because it takes him away from his family too much of the time. Maybe he's already had one heart attack and he is barely fifty. I met such a man who told me he couldn't quit his job because the wife and kids didn't want him to downsize their style of living.

Candice Copeland Brooks and her husband Douglas decided to make a lifestyle change when Doug was averaging twelve hours a day on the job.

"If we had stayed in the city, I could have stayed home. But we decided that was not what we wanted. We made a decision to move to a small mountain town we loved. We started to work together in our company so we could have more time with family."

Doug decided to take the travel burden and do the presentations at fitness events. Candice took on the consulting and writing part of their work to keep her home more. Although the travel took Doug away from the family for part of the month, his overall time with his family was increased.

"Because I was doing most of my end of the business out of our home office, when Doug came home, he was free to spend long days with our children and me."

Many years ago, when I was struggling with the morality of my decision to go to work to help put food on the table, I asked my spiritual advisor if my working outside the home was morally wrong.

I wrote down his words and have tried to use them as my gauge when weighing the many moral decisions I've been faced with as a working mother and wife.

"Morality really comes down to approaching each other (spouses, children, friends, co-workers) with a loving heart."

The wake-up call is a call to love.

His answer really puts the most important issue in the forefront. Our true purpose is to answer only one wake-up call, the call to love, every day of our lives. The challenge we face is to remain aware of those times we respond to each other with less than a loving heart.

The answer always involves pausing, pondering, and making those necessary spiritual, mental, and physical adjustments that allow us to reenter our happiest state of mind, the attitude of gratitude. This book shows you how to repeatedly re-create such a state of bliss in the midst of our multifaceted lives.

CHAPTER TWO

The Gift of Your Presence

Dr. Marel Hanks has side-by-side photos of her son on her desk—at ages six months and twenty-one years.

"I tell the parents of my newborn and toddler patients that the time went so fast, it seems like only two or three years between the dates those photos were taken."

She says babies especially need a mother's close physical presence during the first few years of life. The more time they can spend with them, the better.

"The money they are going to make is not going to replace what they are going to lose with their child."

Pat Mitchell knows she's right. "I regret missing some of those early moments with my son. The first steps, words. Suddenly you wake up, and your baby boy is eighteen."

Whenever you have the opportunity, give your family the gift that keeps on giving: your presence. To be there for your children may entail making temporary career sacrifices. If you already have a good education, marketable skills, and solid work experience by the time your children come on the scene, Judith Regan says you simply make concerted efforts daily to "grab time with your kids." It may mean rocking a few corporate boats.

A FAMILY-FRIENDLY WORK WORLD

Isn't it time working parents get together to create new standards of behavior for ourselves, our families, and our associates in the work world?

Grab time with your children every chance you get.

Terry Savage remembers the time when her son was eleven years old and he had a bad earache. She made a doctor's appointment for him at 10:00 A.M. and wasn't due at work until that afternoon. At 9:15 A.M. she received a call from a man at her television station telling her the governor was about to have a press conference, and she needed to be there by 11:00 to cover it. She told him that she couldn't be there because her son was sick.

"And he told me it was a crisis, and I had no choice."

Then she had a brainstorm. Why couldn't the station send a courier and the crew over to the doctor's office to meet her and her son? The courier could stay with her son and drive him home after the appointment. Then the crew would take her to cover the press conference.

"The desk guy starts yelling at me: 'What do you think this is? A babysitter service?' Then I reminded this bozo that at 6:00 the evening before, when the courier took me home from the station, he had to stop to buy pizzas for the guys at the desk.

"I asked him, 'Is it more of a business thing to pick up pizzas than getting me to this story?' On my day off, no less with a sick son who is supposed to be at the doctor's office?"

The man agreed. The medicine was bought, and her son was dropped off at home. Terry covered the press conference and was back an hour later.

"I realized these guys were asking too much of me. I started playing by my own rules. If they wanted me to be there, then here's how it will come down."

The day Terry Savage took a stand, she raised family consciousness in the workplace for all of us. I have no respect for women who haven't got the guts to keep a commitment to be at a daughter's recital or son's football game, either. Don't they realize it won't get better for all of us if they wimp out?

Pat Mitchell says there was a time when that was easier said than done. "Thirty years ago, when I started in television, I was a single working mother, and we could never discuss our children at work or have pictures of them on the desk. The last thing you wanted was people to know about your kids."

> **Work with and for family-friendly people.**

She remembered going to Boston and interviewing for a job at the local TV station. The man interviewing her practically threw Pat out of his office when he found out she had a five-year-old son. "That was in 1971, but in some business circles, it still goes on. He told me he was not about to hire some twenty-six-year-old mother with a child. According to him, I shouldn't even have been thinking about television. Instead, I needed to go back to teaching or a career that works with motherhood. I left his office in tears."

Pat remembers asking him if he questioned the men he interviewed about whether they had children.

"Of course he said no, because he knew the fellow had a wife."

Slowly, things started changing when "there were greater numbers of women joining the ranks of television talent. Prior to that, it was all we could do to hold our ground and pretend that we weren't women or mothers."

Some of those women became just like the men. "And the rest of us started thinking there was no reason this has to be an antifamily environment. Why couldn't we use our experiences as mothers and family people in the workforce? Then it started translating to the audience on my talk show."

Pat Mitchell was the first woman in national television to have her own show.

"We called it *Woman to Woman*, an all-female company, and all twenty-six women brought their kids to work. The ones who did not have children got pregnant."

Family is your first priority.

Thanks to women like Pat Mitchell, family consciousness is becoming more prevalent in the workforce. Kathie Davis runs IDEA: The Health & Fitness Source, based on a mother and child's best interests. When IDEA's working mothers go home at night, their newborn babies get fresh breast milk because the company provides a "pumping room." The door is often closed throughout the day with a "Do Not Disturb—I Am Pumping" sign on the door.

"Part-time is also common here at IDEA. We have mothers who work two days a week in the office and two at home. Moms who have peace of mind about their children's welfare accomplish more in a few hours than distracted workers do in a week of eight-hour days."

Mothers who work out of their homes two days a week are required to have childcare.

"It's hard to be productive if you are constantly trying to watch your child and finish your work. But with a mother's helper present, it can be perfect."

Kathie Davis knows firsthand that a happy mother makes for an extremely productive employee. Being able to be present periodically throughout the workday with our children is not only beneficial to the families but to a company's overall productivity.

Several companies have changed their attitudes about balancing career and family. One Fortune 500 company is "allowing kids to eat with parents in employee lunchrooms. It also offers one month of paid paternity leave for new fathers, a perk at only twenty-three of the companies on *Working Mothers Magazine*'s list of the top family-friendly places to work."

Hewlett-Packard was listed by the magazine as being one of the pioneer companies in allowing flexible hours. Other more family-oriented environments include "AutoDesk, a software maker in San Rafael, California, that used to have Friday night beer bashes. Now it forgoes the parties and uses the money to help fund employee sabbaticals."

More and more parents are opting to work fewer days a week in the office. It's also encouraging to see a company such as Microsoft, who in the past had one of the best-known reputations as a hard-driving place to work, become so family-friendly.

If you are not in a job situation where they are supportive and understanding, you need to either suggest they test some family-friendly options or have the courage to work elsewhere.

Patti McCord advises, "When I selected IDEA as my employer, the big attraction was not only their work ethic but their family one. Working moms need to ask themselves how the people they work for or with value their own families." Patti believes that a company that puts little or no importance on family contributes to the breakdown of family values in our society.

Work your career around family time.

It helps our case when high profile working mothers choose to spend more time with their children. Two close friends of mine who are talented actresses chose to put their careers on hold during certain growing seasons of their children's lives. They each believe in their talents and know that those talents will not diminish. When the appropriate time comes, they can go back to work.

Up Close and Flexible

Sharon D'Orsie loves hanging out with her children, so she buys real estate based on location—her children's location.

"When I started my business, I bought a fifty-year-old house that was two miles from my office. My boys could ride their bikes there after school. If you can work close to the house, do it."

Judith Regan works close to home, too. "That's how you are able to grab time with your kids. When my daughter gets out of school or has a day off, she comes to work with me. I have a little space for her there, and she draws pictures on paper, makes copies, and runs around the office passing them out and entertaining my staff. Everybody loves her. She helps to create a family environment that helps all of us."

Develop a "make it work" attitude.

Kathy Smith manages to stay close to home and still run a multimillion-dollar operation. She goes in to her company in downtown Los Angeles but mostly works out of her office at home. "I like being able to be there when the kids get home. I really try to balance it so I can spend most of my time in their presence."

When Dr. Roseanne Proteau was a young doctor and a new mother, she took over a pediatrician's practice for a summer while he went to vacation in Europe. "He hadn't had a vacation in thirty-five years. I realized it would have been very difficult for me to raise my family and maintain a balance if I made the choice to have my own practice."

Proteau claims she never made money choices, "only choices that would not sacrifice my motherhood but would still allow me to contribute to the medical profession."

She started working in inner-city clinics with teens three times a week. Then she worked at Misercordia Home for Mentally Handicapped Children.

"I chose to remain on call twenty-four hours a day in order to be with my children. My cousin has a big practice, so my children know I could have made a lot more money making other choices."

Being on call as opposed to having her own practice allowed her to bring her children with her when she made the rounds at the hospital. She was able to volunteer at her children's schools in the morning. This would not have been possible with her own practice. "I always preferred sixty hours a week and maintaining my flexibility. It beats working thirty-five hours a week and putting up with rigidity. And those of us who have worked out more choices for ourselves need to show the other working mothers how they can do it, too."

Ruth Harkin helps other mothers by her example and by always having the courage to speak up and defend the working mom. One time, a group of attorneys and judges were having coffee with her in the law library. They were talking about a person down in Iowa City who brought her baby to work to breast-feed. The woman was a firefighter.

"They were saying how awful that was. They were really downgrading her. And I said, 'What do you guys think I am doing up here?' They said, 'Well, that's different. We know you.'"

Ruth says education and power is what allows us the freedom to make up our own rules.

"When you are the chief law enforcement of a jurisdiction, and you hold the power of indictment, people have a tendency to bite their tongues."

Education is your ticket to spending more time with your family.

When her youngest daughter was born, Ruth was an elected official, and she knew she did not want to take an extended maternity leave. "I did not want to delegate that power to anyone. I was elected by the people, and it was my responsibility to carry on with the duties of my office. So I decided to take my daughter to work with me so I could nurse her. I turned a file room into a nursery."

Bringing her daughter to work was picked up as a newsworthy item by the local morning show.

Ruth said, "Here is this female prosecutor in Iowa taking her baby to work every day. It never occurred to me I was doing an unusual thing. I had two goals: to breast-feed my daughter for a year and be on the job as an elected official. Granted, these goals are not necessarily harmonious."

Ruth said carrying her goals off involved an elaborate system that included packing diapers and bundling up the baby early every morning before leaving for work. Then at 1:00, her neighbor and babysitter would pick the baby up at Ruth's office. In late afternoon, it was back to the neighbor's house to pick up the baby just in time for her late-afternoon feeding.

Flexibility has more value than money for a working mother.

"Moms need to realize they rule the roost when they get educated. It is the ticket to doing whatever you want with your family. Then you create more time with your children by making choices based on flexibility rather than other factors such as money."

Ruth worked at a private law firm for ten years, and there came a time when she had to make a decision on whether to opt for a hard-charging, lucrative law practice or the flexibility to be with her young children. She chose the same option as Dr. Proteau: flexibility. "Some lawyers come into a firm saying they want to work eighty hours a week and make as much money as possible, but I was looking for flexibility. Tom and I had a system of operation we followed, which made it possible to be there for the girls."

Katina Sanderson isn't one of America's 100 most influential women like Judith Regan or Ruth Harkin, but she, too, "grabs time and works it out" to be in the presence of her toddler son, Justin.

I met Katina Sanderson, a Hertz rental agent, at the Twin Falls Airport in Idaho last summer. It was about 3:45 in the afternoon. Nap time. And behind the Hertz counter in the corner, all snuggled up with his blankie and sawing wood to beat the band, was Justin Sanderson. His mother was within eyeshot, sitting at her desk eating a sandwich and doing paperwork.

"Since he's been little, he goes out like a light anywhere. We run the vacuum. Any kinds of noises do not faze him."

What does Justin do when he wakes up?

"He plays with the Avis lady at the next counter."

Katina Sanderson's boss, Betty Gose, the owner of the Hertz franchise in Twin Falls, Idaho, is the kind of mother-friendly supervisor this world needs.

"Justin's grandma helped watch him until she got sick. I told Betty about my babysitting problems, and she suggested bringing Justin to work with me. Betty's a grandma too, so she knows about sitter problems."

Involve the family in your career.

With every career opportunity I've had, I always asked myself how can I keep my children in close proximity to me during my working hours. In spite of no sales training background, I decided to become a salesperson. Selling offered me three options that would benefit my family:

1. The ability to plan my work hours around the family schedule.
2. Money earned commensurate with efforts made.
3. The freedom to have the physical presence of my children in the room as I worked.

I've always walked the tightrope, and I chose the entrepreneurial life. High risk but high reward. My kitchen was my first office. I installed a wall phone with a twenty-five-foot cord in my pantry. This gave me the ability to talk to prospects, stir boiling spaghetti on the stove, and hand a child a carrot, all at the same time. We had a giant plastic laundry basket in the middle of the kitchen floor. It was chock-full of toys.

My kitchen table was huge. On one end of the table, kids would be playing with clay or coloring. On my end, I stuffed my client newsletters into envelopes. Later, the kids earned small change assisting me.

I did all the no-brainer paperwork while they were up and saved work that required concentration until their naptime. I found it to be an effective way to be with my children and teach them about my work.

If this arrangement is too chaotic for your taste, why not do what the IDEA: The Health & Fitness Source moms do? Hire a mom's helper to come into another part of the house while you are on the phones or on the computer.

==I cannot emphasize enough the importance of your physical *presence*, even if it means you run out of your office every hour to dispense hugs and share juice and a cookie together.==

Once your children are in grade school, establish some rules they must follow. I used to tell them that the only way I could stay home and get my work or studies completed was if they were willing to cooperate. This meant no unnecessary interruptions.

I am not suggesting you threaten to abandon them. I made it very clear I preferred doing my work when they were near me. But if I couldn't get my work done, I would be forced to go to my office or the library. I always understood that my presence was as important to them as their presence was to me, so I often used my presence as bargaining power to curtail unnecessary interruptions.

Marel Hanks shared a great "interruption story" with me:

"The hardest thing for me was to tell my kids to leave me alone while I was studying. This one time while I was in medical school, I had three grueling finals on the same day: biochemistry, organic, and calculus. I used to study on this old beat up desk in the dining room that was right by the front door.

She said her house was like the local community center. Kids come in and out all day long, wanting drinks of water or to use the bathroom.

"This particular day, I was very tense. These were very difficult finals, and I was getting nonstop interruptions from these kids. So after about the fifteenth interruption of the day, I shouted, 'No more coming into this house. If you want a drink, use the hose. If you have to go to the bathroom, find a bush. The only reason anybody can come back in will be if you are bleeding. I want to see blood.'"

Five minutes later, her daughter Kendall's best friend Kim came in with a bleeding cut on her finger.

"See, it's blood," said she.

> **Curtail children's unnecessary interruptions during your home work cycles.**

The "show me the blood" story happened well over ten years ago. Today, Kim is a law student at Yale and Dr. Hanks recently got a long-distance call from her. "I have a confession to make," said Kim. "Remember that day you were studying, and I came into your house bleeding? Well, I cut myself on purpose. We all thought it would be very funny. But now I am sitting here, stressed out, trying to study for my finals and asking myself, How did Kendall's mom do it? I do not understand how you took care of your kids and passed those courses. You were and are truly amazing. I just wanted to call and apologize.'"

Marel's eyes filled up with tears at the end of the story. "She understands now."

THE TWO-SIDED EASEL

When Rick Weedn was in kindergarten, he brought home a Mother's Day poem describing what his mom was really like: "She smells like bacon and has paint on her hands."

Artist Flavia Weedn had a passion to become an artist with only one stipulation that it would happen in the *presence* of her children.

"Jack and I were struggling financially. He was selling aerial photos, and didn't like it." Flavia started selling some of her paintings to friends and at shopping mall art shows. "This was going to be our income. If you need money to live on and you think there is even a chance you could make money doing something that you love, you are a fool not to try it. At least try."

She knew that whatever she did to make a living would have to be in the presence of her children. "I needed to do something in my house, or else I never would have done it."

> **Work at home whenever you can.**

Part of her need to be close to her children was born of the pain of losing her first two little boys. She carried them six months and miscarried.

"By the time Rick and Lisa came along, I wanted children very badly. They were both premature. I was grateful that they made it safely into the world. I felt that God had blessed me. They were my miracle gifts, and I was not about to put them in someone else's care. So I had to find a way to make it work with them near me."

She started to paint with her children by her side.

"Lisa was two and Rick was in kindergarten and gone two hours a day. I'd paint something, and it would sell immediately. It got to the point where I wondered how I was going to be able to do this with these two little babies. So I bought a two-sided easel. Up until that point, I didn't even own a single one. I had painted in the bedroom, on masonite, which was propped up on an old trunk and dresser."

Her work time became her time to be with the children, too. "I'd tell them, 'Okay, in one hour when the hand gets to three on the clock we are all going to paint!' They looked forward to this. I have always been very prolific. I could sometimes do four backgrounds at a time while we were all painting together. I didn't realize they were beginning to love it. I just did it as a way for me to get a block of time to paint."

By the time her son Rick and daughter Lisa were in high school, Flavia had her own studio in her house.

"They would walk by when they came home from school. I was always in the studio painting. Rick would make remarks like, 'You need more gold in the right-hand corner because that thing is unbalanced. Now, think, Mom. My eyes are really drawn to the left.' Or Rick would say, 'We need a brochure. And don't use that kind of paper!'"

Then, for a while, the kids rebelled and hated the business, but by the time they were out of college, both of them wanted to be back in their mother's presence doing what they both loved: creating art.

"We hired Rick, then Rick hired Lisa as his assistant."

Today, The Flavia Group is headquartered in Santa Barbara, California, and Rick and Lisa Weedn have managed to get their mother's work licensed all over the world. Now that's presence.

THE WORK CONNECTION

Like Flavia, Jim and Naomi Rhode found creative ways to involve their children in their work.

"Early in our marriage, Jim and I discovered that we were the happiest when we were together. When I started speaking to dental groups on behalf of our company, SmartPractice, I didn't want to speak alone, so Jim joined me on the platform."

In the summertime when the kids were out of school, they all went on the road with Mom and Dad.

"The children wanted something to do on these trips, so they developed a curriculum for a youth program."

All ages at the dental conventions could go hear the Rhode family speak.

"While Jim and I talked to the parents, they did presentations for their children. Eventually, my kids developed a program called 'Teens to the Top' and cut a cassette series that Nightingale Conant distributed for a number of years."

The entire Rhode clan learned one of the toughest of all skills that would serve them well in the future—how to speak in front of an audience—thanks to the dynamic presence of their working mom.

ROAD MOMS

Naomi Rhode packed up her family and took them out on the road with her. So did firefighter and Olympic athlete Cathy Marino Bradford, who begged and borrowed to be able to finance both her son Jared's and her parents' trip to Lake Placid, New York, in July 1992. Cathy was there training with the U.S. Canoe and Kayak Team.

"I couldn't stay away from him that long, so I brought him with me. I rented an apartment, and my parents took care of Jared while I was in training."

Travel with your children.

Nancy Hays is a road mom, too. A singer and a producer, she has worked with some of the biggest names in show business.

"I've watched the super-successful stay on the road and away from their children for months at a time. They end up paying a big price. They are not happy, and they are plagued with family problems. I wasn't going to be one of those parents who are not around while their children grow up."

Nancy says the hard part about traveling with children is the preparation for the trip, which takes plenty of self-discipline.

"Your friends don't make it any easier, either. Everybody is asking me how I expect to be able to drag the baby around and get up on stage and entertain. You must begin every trip in a positive frame of mind. I say to myself, 'I will make this work.'"

Nancy has used her trips as opportunities to bond with each new baby who comes into the family and also spend some quality time alone with her mother. "When my third baby was born last year, I talked my mother into coming on the road with the baby and me. I was producing *The Kenny Rogers Show* for Cardinal Health in Las Vegas."

Her husband is "the perfect partner." She said he picked up the slack with the other two children, which gave him a chance to spend some alone time with the two older kids.

"I was breast-feeding around the clock. We took four days after the show and went back to where my Mom and Dad met. We visited the old hospital where my mother was a nurse. She told me all the old stories of her early life with Dad. It was a wonderful time for her, me, and the baby, with no other distractions. And the show was a big success, too."

I had my sixth child, Kathleen, in the middle of my public speaking career. When she was six weeks old, I took her on the road with me so I could nurse and be with her. I didn't have a problem handling the preparation or extra expense, but the criticism from fellow travelers was tough to take sometimes.

Ninety percent of the time, we flew first class and I was usually the only woman seated in that section; adding a baby to that situation was unique. When Kathleen was four months old, we were flying to a major city and were seated next to a businessman who was an alcoholic. He made my life miserable for four hours, complaining out loud, "I've had a busy day. I cannot understand why the airlines allow this on first class."

While he complained, the stewardess proceeded to serve him over twenty (I counted) vodka tonics. He complained to the guy behind me. Across from me. Anyone who would listen. Meanwhile, Kathleen slept soundly in my arms for four hours without making a peep of noise to disturb this intoxicated executive.

Twelve years later, the first-class section of airplanes is still mostly men, drinking as much as they want, complaining when working mothers bring babies aboard. But we will continue to travel with our children and hope that the airlines and the good old boys network break down and give us the red-carpet treatment we deserve.

There are indications out there that times are changing. A Travel Industry Association of America survey showed that the number of business trips that include children had risen to over 40 million by 1994. In 1990, it was less than 30 million.

With so many more mothers in the workforce, hotels and airlines are becoming more family-friendly. At 100 of the 169 Hyatt Hotels, Camp Hyatt is offered. This includes a bundle of services: babysitting, family activities, supervised programs, and second rooms at half price.

I've heard some mothers say it is too risky to bring a baby along, but where else are we afforded uninterrupted time together? Children also learn how to be very adaptable. Sometimes both stay-at-home and working mothers do not believe in taking their babies out into the world at an early age.

When mothers leave their children home with babysitters, not exposing them to the world until they are almost ready for kindergarten, I notice a big difference in the child's ability to adapt to any situation.

One time I nursed Kathleen in a boardroom before I delivered a proposal to high-level executives of a Fortune 500 company. The men were with the other women and were invited back into the meeting room upon completion of Kathleen's feeding.

The CEO's secretary carried sleeping Kathleen off into her adjoining office. There she slept soundly in her portable crib while I dispensed sales success advice. You've heard it from Ruth Harkin and others and now me. ==Never forget this: When you have the talent, get the education, and earn the work experience that can make you a valuable commodity, you can write your own ticket and go anywhere. Just don't forget to bring along the family.==

I still take Kathleen on several of my business trips each year. Recently, we celebrated her twelfth birthday in New York City. We were also celebrating her good grades. Having the opportunity to travel with Mom is also a strong incentive for maintaining good grades.

Some Working Moms Are Dads

One of our working moms is a dad, and a famous musician who has asked to remain anonymous out of respect for certain members of his family. Let's call him JD (Jazz Dad). Realizing how quickly time flies, JD chose to make some career adjustments while his daughters were still young. Back in the sixties when he was forty years old and at the peak of his career, he fought and won a custody battle for his daughters. His ex-wife was an alcoholic who, on more than one occasion, was too drunk to drive the girls to school.

They were eight and ten years old at the time. "I was forced to reevaluate my career, because I knew the choices: Did I leave my girls with their mother or take custody and hire strangers to raise them?"

But he looked again and found a third choice: "Or should I try to find a way to compromise by cutting back on bookings and take an active role in raising the girls?"

He found a way to include them in his life in a very proactive manner, and he is very grateful he did. He said it takes willpower to turn your back on your career for your children.

"Men have abandoned their families in the past, and now working mothers will be faced with the same temptation unless they say no to work commitments at certain times. That also means coming home from the office and not doing housework all night."

Thirty years later, JD is considered one of the biggest names in the jazz world, and he doesn't feel raising the girls hurt that career one bit, pointing out, "My music is richer and has a depth that comes from experiencing a life of love."

He always had to fight the tendencies to let the help see his daughters more than he did. He admitted that some days he wanted to spend his every waking moment with them and truly understands how mothers feel so torn at times.

He told me there are rhythms in life, just like the seasons of nature. There is a time to work, play, be serious, be crazy. He advises us all to slow down and pace our life with our children's growth. "And if you do, you can still experience everything you ever wanted. When we are young and impetuous, it is so easy to lose sight of the big picture."

JD said that raising kids puts everything in perspective. "Producers and other important people in my life enjoyed working with me because I was not a complainer and I truly feel that comes from the training I received as a father. Parents continually face setbacks and problems, so you grow up fast raising kids."

This jazz legend has influenced other working dads to take custody of their children. "Just because the mother has them doesn't necessarily mean that is where they belong, no matter what the mother's problems are. Fathers miss the experience of a lifetime when they just split and send a check in the mail."

ONLY TEMPORARY

When the late baby doctor Benjamin Spock wrote that mothers should be staying home with their children, he received a flood of letters from working mothers who had to work.

"When I first realized how many mothers were going to work, I figured if they realized how important it was for babies and small children to have a mother at home, they would postpone going to work."

He changed his tune when they wrote him about how guilty he was making them feel. "I wrote parents back that it was important for them to become politically active and vote for candidates who supported subsidized day care so that the mother who has to work can at least be assured that her child is getting high-quality day care while she's away." What about the uneducated, poverty-stricken single working mother? Her challenge is incomprehensible to many of us. She is fighting to change a whole generation, pulling her children out of ignorance and abuse into the world of the educated and free. She must weigh both the short-term and long-term benefits of being separated from her child.

> **Get politically involved if necessary.**

"If that's the case, she needs to be sure her child is in a small and nurturing environment while she has to be gone, always keeping in mind how she can better her situation," says Dr. Marel Hanks.

And that is exactly what working mother Marissa Weaver did. By the time her children were in grade school, she had a college education and a good paying job with plenty of offers for even better ones.

"My plan was always to get in a position to be able to make career choices that kept me in the presence of my children. I paid the price when I worked night shifts and gave up time with my babies to study. Now I try to put myself in situations where I can call the shots."

Presence Implies Commitment

Balancing my act between my family and my career taught me that sometimes the family has to wait and other times the business has to wait. This is a totally acceptable situation for children as long as you continuously prove to them by your actions that your commitments to family hold as much importance in your life as your other commitments.

I've noticed that children do everything they can to work with us, giving us the benefit of the doubt or an A for effort, even when things do not turn out exactly as planned. Natasha McRee, twenty-six-year-old daughter of Heida Thurlow, told me she remembers the conscientious efforts her mother would make to be at her important school events.

All relationships require presence.

"When I was in second grade, my mother drove to school to hear me recite a poem at a school assembly. She was late in arriving and I was the first one to perform, so she missed hearing me. She felt so bad. But I kept telling her how great it was that she dropped everything to get there, knowing how busy she was building the family business at that time."

Natasha said her mother was always far too hard on herself.

"Mom always thought it was important we eat together at night. For us, by the time she got home, we were either starving to death or the family's favorite TV show was on. We would have preferred it if we could have fixed something earlier on our own. Then, when Mom got home, we all could have sat down and relaxed together to watch the show."

Even when Heida was going through chemotherapy for cancer, she made great efforts to keep the family dinner hour intact.

I use to drive mother to her chemotherapy. When we got back, she would try to have dinner with us. But we could see she was just getting sicker. We literally had to force her to go to bed. My mother is a true survivor. She taught me, no matter what, it can be done."

Heida believes "a working mother is constantly looking at her options."

But my children always took priority. Being an entrepreneur gave me that freedom of choice. There is no surefire formula for balancing kids with the career but my rule is: I go by my gut feelings.

"One time my gut told me I really needed to be attending my youngest daughter's track meet because it was more important than being at the gourmet show in San Francisco. That meant so much to her."

> **Honor family commitments as much as you do work commitments.**

On another occasion, when her daughter Natasha was in charge of a large function at her sorority, Heida had a major conflict. It was the first day of a big trade show in Frankfurt. If she had gone to her daughter's function, she would have missed the trade show by three days due to the long travel time.

"My business was at a critical point, and I had to make a decision to go. I explained it to her. I asked her for her advice and together we came to the conclusion that there was no way I could be with her. She knew how hard this decision was for me to make."

Heida said now that her daughter is an adult and working, she genuinely appreciates the fact that her mother financed her college education and realizes the amount of effort that goes into earning that kind of money.

When family commitments are taken just as seriously as professional ones, children learn to trust us and give us some slack when we need it most.

FAMILY GOALS MAKE THE BALANCING ACT WORTHWHILE

When I had to be absent, I got plenty of cooperation by creating exciting family goals. My thirty-year-old son Joe put it like this: "When my Mom was out selling and she was doing really well, she decided we were all going on a ski vacation to Utah. It wasn't like she was out there selling in order to take a vacation on her own. We are a team, and her plan was to take all the members of the team. So, in some ways, I think we were all pushing for her more than she was for herself."

Create family goals.

Valerie Menges says that working has added a few more luxuries to her life that the family truly appreciates: "Travel is one big perk that would not have been available to our family without my job. And the kids knew it and did everything they could not to rock the boat while I was working. Everybody pitched in cooking, etc. Part of that motivation came from them being on the receiving end of the goal.

"When the kids were teens, we focused on vacations that they wanted to take. We went skiing in Colorado. Visited California and Mexico. We knew that our extended time with the kids would soon come to an end, once they focused in on their own lives."

Valerie's oldest son committed suicide a few years later, and his girlfriend told her that he frequently talked about how much the family vacations meant to him.

"We had good talks around the campfire. I miss my son terribly, but I hold on to those special times together."

Just Say No

Being present for your children means learning to know when to draw the line and say no. Otherwise, you can seriously jeopardize the trust that exists between you and your child. Senator Robert Dole's chief of staff, Sheila Burke, struggled with that issue with her son.

During the week of the welfare debate, Sheila blocked off one night as sacrosanct to fulfill a long-standing promise to take her son to a Yankees game in Baltimore. He marched into her office at the appointed hour with his father, his cap, and a question: "Are you going with?" The welfare bill was still on the floor; Sheila was stuck in the office.

"No," she told him.

"Good," he said. "I hate you."

"I know you don't mean that."

"Yes, I do."

"There's just no way to not feel guilty," Sheila groaned, vowing to find tickets if the Yankees made the playoffs.

Granted, there are times when promises are broken. As Heida said, we have to know when we have gone too far. I remember the day that I made the "Say No" commitment to myself.

One Halloween morning, I had to make a presentation in upstate New York. I agreed to do it because, due to the time change, I thought I could get back to California in time to trick-or-treat with my children.

> **Say no to distractions that take you away from family and work.**

Halloween may not be a big deal to everybody, but for me it ranks as one of my all-time favorite holidays. Ever since the children were babies, I have dressed up in goofy costumes and paraded down the neighborhood streets with my crew begging for candy with the best of them.

The flight I was due to take was canceled, and I couldn't get out of New York until late that afternoon. I had several hours to kill, so I went to a coffee shop. At about 3:00 P.M. while sipping my second cup, I looked out the window on an especially clear and colorful fall day. First-grade kids in costumes were marching past the window with their teacher on the way to their bus stop.

My heart sank. I got so homesick for my trick-or-treaters, I started to cry. I made a commitment that day to "just say no" if my work left me alone and homeless on future Halloween nights.

Janice Fuchs is constantly saying no in order to keep her priorities straight.

"I sacrifice leadership positions and invitations to sit on boards of directors. Sometimes I think to myself that it sounds sexy to be on this board or co-chair that gala event. And it is flattering to be asked. But I also know that it means more early-morning or late-afternoon meetings. Those are times I spend with my children."

While raising all my children, I became very selfish about my time. I was often asked to chair golf tournaments or become a volunteer. I always figured I could do that later in life. And that is exactly what has happened. I now do lots of volunteer work for a theatre group entitled Company of Fools in Hailey, Idaho. But the time is right. We all need to be sensitive to timing. If we are and if we learn to wait on some of those dreams we wish to pursue, the opportunity will present itself at the perfect moment. And it will be a joy instead of an additional burden.

WHO NEEDS A SOCIAL LIFE?

Being present for our children requires a certain exclusivity. I must admit that my social calendar has been pretty empty over the last thirty-two years. Most of the friendships Mike and I have formed are an extension of the life we share with our children.

Mike and I know that when our last child, Kathleen, goes off to college, we can devote more time to friends. Most working parents who are effectively raising their children and tending to their careers are not social butterflies.

Dr. Roseanne Vitullo Proteau credits her success at juggling family and career to "keeping my socializing to a minimum. My husband thought I was going through puberty instead of menopause because I loved hanging out with my teenage daughters and their friends. I took twenty girls up to Lake Geneva for a two-night sleep over during Christmas vacation one year."

Socialize selectively.

Roseanne killed two birds with one stone: cutting back on her social calendar to be available for her children and getting to know exactly who her children's friends were.

I've always recognized the importance of peer influence on my children, particularly from middle school to college. Because I am a working mother, I need to pay close attention to who my children are socializing with, especially when I am away.

Keeping up with your children's friends must be an ongoing process. I've seen parents do all the right things to bond with their little ones, but they lose track of who their children's friends are as they get older. Then, suddenly, the least likely child in the family, the one who was mother's little darling as a toddler, gets involved with the wrong crowd. And any good influence that the child received early in life is wiped out. Never underestimate the power of a negative friend's presence in your child's life, particularly from middle school age on up.

Parents who encourage their kids to invite friends over on the weekend can learn a lot about who they pal around with at school. We owned ski boats and sailboats for most of the children's growing-up years, and while all of our friends were out playing golf, we took our gang and many of their friends on excursions to Catalina Island, Lake Mead, and even to the Caribbean.

There were snow skiing holidays, fishing trips, lots of dinners out at restaurants, and trips to the local ice cream parlors sometimes three nights a week. It was almost standard procedure to see us walking into a restaurant with fifteen kids on a Saturday night and then after dinner, catching a movie.

We don't have a fat savings account today because, besides financing six children (so far) through college, we spent a lot of money and time on them and their friends during some critical growing years. But those were some of the greatest times we've had together. I know for many families, that was not the case. The teen years were a nightmare. If you work and have a heavy social calendar, when are your children going to be blessed with your presence?

THE GOOD OLD MOMMY NETWORK

Having a social circle that centers around our children has many side benefits. Entertainer/producer Nancy Hays tells a story that proves you do not have to be in a business environment to make deals or advance your career.

"Guys do it on the golf course. Working moms do it at their children's birthday parties."

Do what? Networking, of course. She happened to be at the same birthday party as a very successful businesswoman. Their daughters were in the same preschool.

"All the kids were running wild, and we started to talk. She told me she was a product manager. In the midst of all the chaos, screaming kids, and balloons popping, she gave me a tip about who to call in her company who handles name entertainment for the annual meetings.

"We had a more productive business meeting at a Saturday afternoon kids' birthday party at Lincoln Park Zoo than all the men do at their wasted business lunches. But the best part was, I did all this in the presence of my child."

Present in Spirit

Although we constantly strive to include ways to be physically present with our children, that is not always possible. For those times when we all wish we could be together, we can teach them another way to make that happen.

Patti McCord taught her little daughter Amanda "that even though we are apart, we are always together. I think of her all day long while I am at work. I tell her I do, and she will recite that back to me. I will say, 'Amanda, I am really sorry it was such a long day today.'

"And she will say, 'Mom, we were in each others hearts.'"

We are the ones who set the tone when we leave our children to go to work in the morning. Amanda is only four, but she understands the meaning of being close to her mother in more ways than one.

"Amanda trusts me. She knows when she needs me, I am there physically, and we are always together in some form, which is so comforting and peaceful for a child. Parents should train them young to see that."

I'm glad I did. Because the greatest gift a mother could receive is to know that her presence was not only appreciated by her children, but it made a difference in their lives. My son has not only given me that gift but sent it in a letter to me on the occasion of his twenty-fourth birthday. I will cherish his words for the rest of my life:

> *I have been so fortunate to be overwhelmed with that feeling of togetherness, which is the gift of family. And while physically we may be miles apart, in my heart I feel this family all the time. The love, the tightness, the strength. We all feel it.*
>
> *And you, my dear mother, are the source. Your energy has a captivating force about it. And with each of your children, we take that energy with us in the pursuit of our own dreams,*

happiness, and goals. I am so glad that I was born to you, so I could be in your presence to get to know you and love you.

Our presence is the most important gift we bestow on our children. When I asked Susan Gamba how she wanted to be remembered after her life here was over, her answer impressed me more than any other mother I interviewed. Her words describe the monumental impact someone's presence can have on our lives. "I want to be missed terribly. I want everybody to have the biggest hole in their heart, thinking, 'God, I am not going to be able to see, hear, or talk to her again.'

"I think if you go that way, then you have really touched a lot of people's lives."

CHAPTER THREE

Abolishing Slavery

While their unemployed husbands are doing no more than 36 percent of the housework, a recent study on "high stress and high shame" reported that women "who bring home the bacon are really expected to fry it, too."

Anytime someone accepts being treated like a slave as a way of life, it is very stressful. And shame on those perpetrators of slavery.

"I see now I made life tough on myself," says Shirley Pepys. "My married daughter Rene has made me realize the women in my generation must have silently agreed to be treated like slaves."

Rene owns her own company. Shirley gets to observe firsthand how her daughter handles the juggle between career and family quite differently than she did.

"What an eye-opener this has been for me," says Shirley. "Rene's attitude about taking care of herself is a given. She has no guilt about things I agonized over. She just went on a girls' weekend. Her husband Stan watched my granddaughter Catherine. But I was the one thinking to myself, 'How can you go? You just got back from a business trip.'"

Rene says it's easier for her to delegate, and she refuses to go on those guilt trips her mother took while she was growing up. But Shirley believes her daughter's assertiveness has a lot to do with her son-in-law.

Delegate, delegate, delegate.

"Her husband does not see her work or going off with the girls as a take-away from him. Men in my generation felt the time not devoted strictly to them was a waste of time. They demanded our attention, and we figured we had no choice but to jump through hoops. We spoiled them rotten. But let's face it, so did their mothers."

Mothers spoiling sons is precisely the problem, according to Olga Silverstein, author of *The Courage to Raise Good Men*. "Women divorce a man because he's self-centered, doesn't relate well, doesn't understand what intimacy means, he can't talk, and he's not in touch with his feelings. WE RAISED THOSE MEN. Women did that. It's time to start at the beginning. Let's not raise them so we have to fix them later."

TO HONOR AND RESPECT ONE ANOTHER

We may all need "fixing," because when honor and respect are lacking in a relationship, somewhere in the course of it, the two people must have agreed to lower their standards and expectations. So how do we begin to fix the problem?

"Train the men to behave," says Judith Regan. "'If we don't, we will continue to have a culture of women running themselves ragged trying to do everything. Look at neighborhoods where mothers are left with no money, trying to raise kids in violent areas."

It's not just the men who need training. "Women must learn how to say no to sexual promiscuity. We must get together collectively. None of us can do this by ourselves. If we don't set a standard to be treated with dignity and respect together, then he won't have to behave and will be able to go next door to get what he thinks he wants. In fact, men are more satisfied, ultimately, if they have a standard set that they can measure to," says Regan.

When we accept such behavior from men, it not only demoralizes us but also dehumanizes men, turning them into irresponsible inseminators. What happens, says family psychologist Judith Wallerstein, "is everybody forgetting that the children who result from these indiscretions are human beings who need parenting to survive. They're not like puppies. They are very much in need, and they know that. If they are not taken care of, they'll die."

Don't lower your moral standards.

Some men and women have a terrible fear of being alone. This fear motivates them to make poor moral judgments. Regan says a woman who fears being alone rationalizes, "None of the men are behaving, so I have no choice but to be with an amoral man."

Regan's own family influenced her strong opinions regarding her expectations of men. "I had a wonderful father and brothers. These are nice men and quite frankly, I was shocked when I found out men outside of my family were not like my father and brothers. My mother was honored and respected in our home."

If human decency is lacking in the relationship with a man, Regan advises living alone.

"The truth is you are more alone in a relationship with a man who mistreats you than you would be if you drew the line and defined your boundaries. Men need and respect a woman who demands to be treated with respect."

Those were Ruth Harkin's exact sentiments when she first started dating her husband Tom. She knew that being treated without honor starts when women silently and routinely accept small acts of inconsideration as part of normal routine in a relationship.

It takes courage to let the guy who you are falling in love with know you do not appreciate nor intend to put up with his selfishness. But Ruth called him on it, and Tom respected her for delivering the message so much so that he still tells the story thirty years later with a great deal of relish.

"Something happened when I first met Ruth that indicated to me this is the kind of person I would like to marry. I was still in the navy. She had just gotten out of the army, and we were starting to date one another. This one time she came over to visit me in Japan, so I set up a double date with a buddy of mine and his girlfriend.

Honor and respect one another.

"We two guys had a little time to kill before we were to meet the gals, so we went over to the O club and we got to drinking. You know, just a bunch of us pilots talking. Well, time slipped away, and I showed up two and a half hours late for our date."

Tom started joking around about being tardy, but Ruth didn't see much humor in his behavior.

"I didn't pay much attention when she stood up and walked over to the kitchen to get a kettle of water. Then she just walked over to me and poured it right over my head, saying, 'You know, you think you just can do that. Well, you can't do that to us.'"

Tom had on a brand new sport jacket, which got soaking wet.

"But that was Ruth. And the stage was set. She put my feet on the ground. I realized I was not some hotshot navy pilot that could treat women like they were playthings.

"When that happened, I knew her maybe five months. No one had ever done that to me before. I had always gone out with women who were very acquiescent. Those who sort of let the man do whatever he wants. I thought what Ruth did was pretty good. Here is a pretty strong woman."

Assert and Train

By calling Tom on his thoughtlessness, Ruth taught him an important rule: "I expect the best, and when I don't receive it, you will hear about it." It's not wrong to expect the best when you are willing to give the best, too. Remember, Ruth was on time. Tom was the tardy one. Ruth trained her man early by asserting herself.

My husband, Mike truly believes men, especially, need to be taught decent behavior. He has been advising our daughters for years that if they expect to end up with a true partner, then they better train their boyfriends right up front.

Assert with love and kindness.

And if you are already married and not getting much cooperation, Mike advises you to "speak up. Some men are terrible mind-readers. Be assertive. You must tell us what you want in a loving manner. Some women gunnysack by not asking for what they need and stifling their anger. Then, seemingly out of the blue, they explode. Asking for anything should become a regular habit."

The first time I heard Mike talking about training a man, he was giving a sales meeting to a group of high-powered but stressed-out saleswomen who were burning the candle at both ends. And I happened to be one of them at the time. I taped his speech:

> *I don't understand this. If I were to combine the incomes of all of the women in this room, they would be in the billions. You are the best of the best. So, what's the problem? I notice that you are not getting the cooperation at home that you all deserve.*
>
> *You are rushing out of the office like nervous wrecks, telling me you have to put dinner on the table at a certain time or your spouse and children will hit the roof. Not to mention the*

other demands that you allow to be put on you: packing lunches for able-bodied children, making their beds, picking up trails of their dirty laundry.

If they won't pick up after themselves, why don't you hire someone to come in to clean, do the laundry, and iron? Look at the six-figure incomes you are making. Don't tell me you cannot afford help. One of you gave me a poor excuse, saying you do not feel like you are being a proper wife or a mother unless you do these things. Some of you are guiltily asking your husbands to watch the children when you get called out to close a deal as if they were babysitters. Hel-lo. This is their dad, ladies.

I taped Mike's "Train a Man; Free a Slave" speech for posterity. Then I asked him to marry me. Pure genius, huh?

Free the slave that's within you.

Mike's talk centered around the extra physical burdens women carry. Privately, he shared stories with me about their emotional burdens, too. One night when we were out to dinner, having one of our heart-to-heart talks, I complimented him on his sensitivity toward women. He told me how his lack of it in one particular woman's case helped him become more understanding.

"One of my top saleswomen really took a dive in her production right after she won the yearly top producer recognition award. I jumped to conclusions and thought she was becoming complacent. One day, when I wrongly accused her of letting success spoil her attitude, she blurted out the real reason for her sudden lack of productivity." It seems the woman was continually sacrificing her own career desires to keep peace in her home. Just as she reached some impressive goals on her job, her home life seemed to fall apart. She told Mike that her husband turned cool and condescending. "The guy was an expert in dampening her spirits at peak moments of her career."

For example, when Mike notified her that she was the number-one saleswoman in the company for the year, he had no idea of the hell she would have to pay.

The award would be presented at the annual sales meeting, which was out of town. Of course, her husband had no time to go with her. So on the way to dropping her off at the airport, he couldn't resist yet another opportunity to burst her bubble. "You really think you are Miss America these days, don't you?"

It was not only her husband's remarks that ultimately killed her spirit. Her children picked up their father's resentful attitude and treated their mom with the same lack of respect. Yet all of the family seemed to enjoy the fruits of their mother's success: private-school educations, braces on their teeth, and memberships in prestigious country clubs.

On her way to receive an award that should have been the highlight of her career, this woman felt guilt-ridden and sick at heart. Thus, in the months following, her productivity took a sharp decline.

Grown-Ups with a Clue

In-house slavery is never a problem in homes where boys and girls were taught to gradually take over the responsibility of looking after themselves. Choosing a self-sufficient partner will make life much easier for a future working mother. I think it is important for young women reading this book to become aware of how so many of the husbands of working mothers were self-starters. It certainly should be one of the valuable qualities a woman looks for in a future husband.

Don't sweat the small stuff.

Tom Harkin's mother died when he was ten years old and when his father was sixty-four and in ill health.

"I had to fend for myself. We were a very poor family. All during high school, I made my own lunches. Every Saturday morning, I would wash the clothes and hang them out on the line. Not only clothes, but my sheets, and I had to iron everything. I made meals, too. I love to cook, and now it is one of my forms of relaxation."

Tom went to live with a sister who forced him to take care of himself. He also had to help clean her house.

"My sister was old-fashioned just like my immigrant mom. She's the one who taught me how to clean a house. I couldn't go anywhere until I washed dishes, vacuumed, and did my wash. Pitching in was instilled in me at a very young age."

Patti McCord's husband Greg had no choice but to cooperate at his house, too. His mother was the accountant in the family business.

Patti cannot imagine being in a relationship where the partner refuses to do something or lacks flexibility. "But I also know I would not have fallen in love or married someone who showed signs of inflexibility. In dating, you try to give and take. When the other person is not terribly giving, that's a pretty good sign that it is time to end it."

McCord believes her life works because she and her husband Greg love each other and went into the relationship wanting it to be successful.

Become a team player.

"We are a team. I wash my own car. I mow the lawn. He changes diapers. He cooks dinner. Sure there are things I do regularly like keeping up with the laundry. Nothing is always one person's job around here. We trade things off."

She says neither of them spend time letting the little things bother them. "I know, for example, that Greg hates to sort socks that come out of the dryer. That is not a problem for me, but being faced with a poopy diaper when I come in the door after work is."

The willingness to do what it takes to make the family run smoothly is an asset. If either partner lacks willingness to do a particular duty, then Patti says, "Bottom line, either you do it or hire someone else to do it. Then let it go. Far too much time is wasted on blame, performing certain functions with an angry heart. That mind-set is terribly destructive."

Both parents have certain needs that cannot be overlooked. It is important that each of us as partners know what those critical needs are. For example, Patti McCord must take time to get up and run at 5:00 A.M.

"That means Greg has to get the kids up, dressed, off to the babysitter and school. I hear my friends say their husbands would never do that. Well, he has to. It is not an option for him to say, 'Gee I would rather not do that.'

It is just part of the deal. I don't demand it. I just got in the habit of doing it. Then it becomes an unspoken expectation. He has the same unspoken expectations that I fulfill. I am home a lot at night and he is not there. He is a pastor of a church and going to school, working on getting a master's degree. To be successful means to accommodate each other whenever possible."

Sharing responsibilities becomes normal when both spouses are assertive about what they will do or about what they need. All requests are made in a kindly manner. It's also important to be sensitive and aware of how each partner feels on a given day.

Be sensitive and aware.

"Maybe you have a deal with Dad that when he comes home at night, he gives the children their bath. But if he has had one of those harrowing fifteen-hour days and is on his last legs, giving a toddler a bath may be nothing but a hassle," says Candice Copeland Brooks.

A better solution on that particular night might be for Mom to give the bath and Dad could read the bedtime story.

Strict policies do not always work. "'Everybody must feel their way through and see what works best for their family," says Candice.

Janice Fuchs says, "It's no accident that I am married to the type of man that I am. One of the reasons I picked him was I knew from the beginning he would be an equal partner." Her husband was willing to move to a different place when she was offered the promotion with Rouse and the opportunity to relocate to Newport Beach.

"Our son was only five months old at the time. My husband went to his company, Merrill Lynch, and asked for a transfer so I could accept the promotion.

Help others grow.

"I owe a lot to my husband's mom. She raised him to be a wonderful helpmate. He is very task-oriented and very responsible. We sat down during our courtship and discussed exactly what kind of a life we wanted. The kind of parents we would be. Who would do what, and how we both would help each other grow and share the parenting responsibilities. I knew what I was getting into with him."

It's never too late to ask for what you need. When Valerie Menges's children were fifteen and seventeen years of age, she was running the family business. There were weaknesses in the business that centered around accounting and business planning. She wanted to go back to college, knowing if she gained knowledge in those areas, the business would benefit. Valerie signed up, and her husband took care of the kids and also prepared or brought home dinner.

"I left for school at 5:00 A.M. and got home by 6:30 P.M. in the evening. Getting that education paid off big time in our family business. Profits doubled because I became a master of good accounting principles."

Sometimes a spouse must jump in out of necessity, and the payoffs are both rewarding and surprising. Sara Wilsensky's husband discovered a talent he didn't know he had when their children came along.

"It is the same at home as it is in the rest of the world. People are not motivated by what you think or what you need. They are motivated by what they think and what they need. So what would be helpful is to say something that would change the way your spouse thinks or responds to a need he has.

"That is what happened to my husband David. He needed to know that the baby would be breast-fed because he was a big believer in it. And he needed to know the mother of his baby would not wither away. So he responded to that need."

When their first child was born, David noticed that when Sara came home from work at 5:00, instead of making dinner, she immediately started nursing the baby. The baby's dinner was the only one Sara could deal with when she first got home.

"David is a bright person. So he figured out if he wanted to eat, he would have to do something. He also noticed I was not eating, either. If he started to cook, we would both eat and consequently, it would be better nourishment for all three of us."

This started the Wilsenskys on quite a gourmet eating expedition with Dad.

"David is now a full chef. He makes his own homemade pasta and sauce. He had no interest in cooking until the baby was born. It all started because we all needed a meal."

Sara said he never complained, "Why aren't you making dinner?"

He was more concerned that the baby would have breast milk and Sara would get enough nourishment for both herself and the baby. Now, he not only cooks but plans the meals a week ahead of time and does the shopping. He washes all the dishes, too, and loads and unloads the dishwasher.

Nancy Hays's husband learned how to be self-sufficient growing up in a big family. I am grateful to my in-laws for the way they raised my husband. If I find out I have to perform in Chicago or Las Vegas next Friday night, my husband jumps in to help out enthusiastically. He doesn't say, 'No, you cannot do that.' Or 'four kids are going to suffer.' We make it work with a combination of his help and a great babysitter."

Nancy Hays needs to know her husband is in her corner more than anything, especially during high-pressure times in her career.

So did Tracy Thompson. When she was appointed to be the head of the Small Business Administration a few years back, her two sons stayed with her all summer in Washington, D.C., but then went back in the fall to Minnesota with her ex-husband. Each of them, at some time throughout the year, had to be both mother and father to their children.

Was her ex-husband resistant when she got her call from the President of the United States and was required to relocate?

"No, and at first, I assumed he was supportive because he had to be, because it was when he took the prosecutor's job."

Earlier in their marriage, they lived in rural Winona, Minnesota. Tracy's ex-husband Jeff moved the family from there to Faribault, Minnesota, where he became the vice county prosecutor. This meant they took the boys away from all of their cousins, aunts, and uncles. And the move took Tracy away from her work as the small business development director for Winona State University.

Shortly after she was appointed to the Small Business Administration, there was a woman in that arena who wrote a note to someone on staff that Tracy happened to read. It stated that any mother with two small children who accepted Tracy's position must have no family values. How could she possibly leave her little ones to take such a job?

"Her remarks hurt me so much, I almost packed my bags and went home." Tracy started thinking maybe the woman was right. Perhaps she was a bad mother.

"The only thing that saved me was my ex-husband. He reminded me that there were men who leave their states to go to D.C. for public service or people who go to war. He said when that happens everybody just makes the necessary sacrifices."

Jeff told Tracy it is unfortunate that when men go to Congress, nobody questions their decision. But that is not always the case with women. He felt it was important for her to know that the family was 100 percent behind her and willing to sacrifice.

"Once I wondered if he was doing this because he really thought he owed it to me because I stood behind him when he wanted the prosecutor's job. But then I found out that he was very proud of me. He could have easily made me feel guilty and agreed with the woman. But he never thought to say, 'You know, you should be home with these kids, so get your butt over here and warm up some chicken.'"

When you marry your best friend, you end up with what my daughter and her friends call a "real dude." According to the daughters, a dude is a cool guy because he can hammer a nail or change a diaper. He may be a tough prosecutor in a courtroom but at home he's a pussycat as he whips up huevos rancheros on Saturday morning or takes charge as his wife flies off to Bosnia to negotiate a peace treaty.

Recently, I spoke to an audience of 3,000 home-based working mothers who sell clothing for an organization called The Weekenders. As I prepared my speech, I was amazed at the statistics I read from their organization. Thousands of these women earn six-figure incomes. I also had the opportunity to see many of their husbands at the convention. They were pushing baby strollers around and having their own "spouse sessions" on how to be more supportive partners.

At their evening awards banquet, the husbands of the year's top producers seemed genuinely thrilled for their successful wives' accomplishments. I talked to many of the men who felt they had the best of both worlds: more time with family and more money. One dad said, "It used to mean more income meant I spent less time with my family.

But now that my wife is an entrepreneur, that's no longer true."

During my speech, I took the opportunity to recognize all these great men in the audience, referring to them as "true dudes." I asked them to please stand so all of their wives and I could applaud them and show our genuine admiration. We women cheered them for their courage to break out of the macho loop of life while the song "We Are Family" blasted throughout the hall. The place went wild.

NEW FAMILY LIFESTYLES

So you say you are looking for a real dude to free you from slavery once and for all. Do you know that will mean giving up some of your male fantasies? Are you willing to give up certain ideas regarding what makes him sexy, attractive, and valuable as a human being? Are you ready to quit stereotyping like the rest of your girlfriends do?

Terry Savage says, "What some of us really need is a man who acts like a wife. We say we want help and equal partners, but when the men we love are the type to change diapers or have a job with the flexibility that allows them to bake cookies for our children's second grade Valentine's Day party, it's a turnoff."

Value a man for his character not his bank balances.

Terry said she was once married to her so-called fantasy guy. He was a CEO who she traveled with internationally as his trophy wife. "I missed my TV show, my business, my friends, and my separate life.

"After that divorce, I dated a guy I knew I would never marry. He was an electrician by trade. The most charming, wonderful guy I have ever been with. He revolved his life around me and my son. Driving my son to the pool and soccer games; cooking dinner for us. While we were dating, everybody laughed at me. My friends kept asking me what I was doing with this person. What I was doing with him was having a wonderful life. He adored me and my son. He made our life so much easier. Later, when I broke up with him, I got very sick."

Terry said she was raised believing she should marry someone who was equally or more powerful than she was. "But I can see how shallow my thinking has been. I had lunch with a high-powered female executive the other day who has a wife for a husband. He plays tennis with the kids in the afternoon. But she was so happy, and it's what makes their life work."

Kathy Smith says it takes hard work before you reach that level of happiness and spiritual satisfaction with your mate. She shares the changes she and her husband Steve went through. "I was a millionaire by the time I was thirty-two. My fitness videos were going gangbusters and consistently in the top five on the charts along with Jane Fonda's tapes. My husband had a great job with a more-than-respectable salary, but it was no comparison to what was coming in on my end."

Then Kathy got pregnant.

"We asked who was going to be the parent that would stay home once the baby arrived. Neither of us necessarily had to stay home, but we agreed that it would be in our baby's best interest. Steve and I wanted children badly. We both felt strongly that we did not want our children raised by nannies."

So when Kathy had the baby, they decided Steve should quit his job. "This was a mutual decision. He was ready because he was tired of the travel. So he quit and helped me with my business."

But like Terry Savage, in Kathy's girlhood fantasies the man was supposed to take care of the woman financially. Now she was the breadwinner, and her husband was staying home with their child while she traveled on business. She loved her family and her work passionately, but there was some struggle inside herself she did not fully understand right away. She was being tested on a higher, more spiritual level. When we find our true partners in life, we must be willing to throw out our false sense of values.

"My husband is a man all my girlfriends wished I could clone. We have this mommy group at my daughter's school. I sit in there and listen to these women complain about their husbands. These women do not work, and they complain that they have the children twenty-four hours a day and their husbands never lift a finger. I cannot relate."

Kathy now appreciates Steve as her full partner, but "it took plenty of good communication during long walks. My father died when I was seventeen, and two years later, my mother was killed in a plane crash. I was able to heal because Steve was willing to listen to me work through my abandonment issues."

"Steve has his own travel club business now, but he can still set his own hours. The burden is never on one person in our home. Recently, my daughter Katie came down to visit me in Orlando where I was doing a keynote address for the Women's Sports Foundation. We were going to do Epcot and the Kennedy Space Center together.

"Steve was in California, preparing her. He took her shopping, and he knew just where to go. The Gap. Nordstrom's. He is so practical. Made sure she had a backpack so she wouldn't have too many things to carry. Bought her the right socks, shorts, and tops. She arrived with all the right stuff, her books, homework, and even a present for me. Other moms say their husbands would not have a clue."

Smith says she finally realized that she found what she was looking for all along. "Steve is better than a fantasy. He is real."

We were raised to respect and often are attracted to men who have a deep work ethic but absolutely no sensitivity as a husband or a father. Women who marry these ambitious souls often end up out in the cold and constantly questioning their own worth as a human being.

A working mother in the computer field who asked to remain anonymous told me, "I belong to a group of mothers who meet every Friday night. I am the only working mom in the group. At first, I felt very self-conscious and guilty around them. As the group unfolded and we all got to know each other, I began to feel much different.

"These women are trying to discover their own value, even though they are good mothers. Their husbands are all very big dealers in town. They put pressure on their wives like you would not believe. They want to know if their wives are growing. One woman put on some weight, and her husband wanted to know why she wasn't exercising.

"There is one lady in the group who was formerly a successful decorator. She didn't have her first child until she was thirty-seven. She has a real problem asking her husband for help with the baby. She feels like he is making all the money, so she better shut up. He plays on that big time. Recently, he told her she could not have a housekeeper unless she does decorating consulting one hour a week to pay for the maid. I would not want to be in any one of these women's shoes."

Janice Fuchs is in her mid-thirties and always knew she wanted a career. She isn't as confused as some of us who grew up with the Prince Charming fantasy. She was smart enough to notice many additional qualities besides her husband's potential earning capacity. "Too often, our criteria for choosing a mate or living happily with our spouse is power and money."

It's going to take time to remove the negative stigma connected with men who stay home, even though the benefits of a child being cared for by a parent generally far exceeds day care supervision. Being a househusband is another family option many couples choose. John Konihowski, a former wide receiver with the Edmonton Eskimos and the

Winnipeg Blue Bombers, is married to Diane Jones Konihowski, Canada's top track and field star in the seventies, who is currently vice president of the Canadian Olympic Association, and who made over fifty out-of-town trips last year.

"We felt, why have kids if you're not going to take care of them?" says John.

Hire and train.

Househusbands result from many factors. In the last three decades, layoffs have hit men harder. These layoffs have been targeted to males in middle-management positions and manufacturing jobs. Also, many wives are now earning more than their husbands, and the couple agrees they want to have one parent at home.

Finding and Training the Help

We have spent most of this chapter talking about finding and training grown-up men in order to abolish slavery in the home. But some working mothers freed themselves from slavery by simply hiring outside help. Their spouses weren't the Mr. Mom types, and training them to become such types would entail a lobotomy. Here's how Joanne Konz explains her situation. "My husband came from a totally different background than I did. My dad worked all day and came home and helped my mother all night. On the other hand, my husband's family were farming types. And those boys were never required to do anything. Their mother waited on them hand and foot, and she realizes now that has presented a problem."

Joanne said there was a period of time when she would come home and feel like it was still her responsibility to do the cooking and cleaning up after supper.

"My husband is one of those people who will eat and leave the table and go sit in front of the television. For a long time, I was angry about that. I was getting nowhere saying anything. But I also knew he was my best friend and the world's greatest dad, who simply loved to go out and play with his children every chance he got."

She figured if she couldn't train him, she would hire someone she could train. And that's exactly what she did. "Now I get to go out and play with them, too.

"I don't get all bent out of shape over the little things. Being a great partner doesn't necessarily mean he always picks up his dirty socks and empties the trash without being asked. I can hire people to do those chores. Money can't buy the emotional support my husband gives me."

Even if your husband is a "dude," like my husband Mike is, it's very difficult to juggle family and career without some outside help. Once I finally broke down and realized we needed help, I had to overcome another problem that I find typical among working mothers.

One Friday morning, I was running the vacuum before 7:00 A.M. Mike walked into the living room half asleep and wondered what the heck I was doing.

"Tidying up a bit," say I.

"Isn't it a little early?" says he.

"I have to do it before the cleaning lady gets here."

Sound familiar? Only a working mother could turn into her cleaning lady's employee. I had to be reminded that I hired them to work for me. If you have a similar problem, make yourself sit down and write a job description or a list of duties. Then tell the help nicely what you expect. Mike would say it's all about assertion without anger.

Have you ever pulled these doozies on yourself?

- Hiring someone too fast and discovering they are not a good fit with the family, then allowing them to hang around until things get nasty.

- Not taking the time to train the helper thoroughly and then gunnysacking anger again because we are doing jobs we expect the help to do. But of course the help has never been told or trained to do said job.

Many of our working moms have solved the previous dilemmas. Paula Perry and her husband Keith approach the interviewing and hiring of babysitters with the same formality and thoroughness they use with the employees at their restaurant. "It's getting that right fit. We interview many people before we make our choice. Too many times, people stop interviewing too soon and take the first person who comes along." They always get plenty of references and rely heavily on word of mouth. "We try to eliminate surprises that can come up later, so we find out about the person's family life. Are they stable people? If we've never had the opportunity to see this person in other working situations, we talk to people who have. Being able to trust someone is critical."

Heida Thurlow made it her mission to find the right person the first time to take care of her children. She says you simply cannot settle for someone who is not right for your family. She has a good track record because of her thorough hiring policies. Most of her family's and company's support team stayed with her for several years.

"Once you find the right person, you pay them well. And you make them part of your family. That may involve learning their language and taking the needs of their family into consideration. My assistant leaves the office a half hour early three days a week so she can pick up her children from day care."

Sharon D'Orsie's number one financial priority has always been budgeting for a first-class housekeeper. "It costs me twice as much on an annual basis to maintain my housekeeper than to make the total house payments. Believe me, you will find good people when you are willing to pay them."

She prospected for such help through local churches, schools, a network of friends, and agencies. When she found the perfect fit for her and her sons—a widow with five grown children—she treated her just like any other member of the family.

Whenever Sharon had the day off, her housekeeper would get the day off. Whenever Sharon had a vacation, the housekeeper took a vacation, too.

"If she wanted to visit a daughter or friend, all she had to do was let me know way ahead of time. Then it would be worked out. I always gave her the respect this position deserved."

Sharon's helper was with her for over ten years, but Janice Fuchs has some reservations about keeping the same person for so long. "Even if you find the right person the first time, that person may not be the right fit for your child in two more years. If I had to do it over, and assuming I had good references, I would choose caregivers whose age suits my child's development."

When the baby is sleeping and eating most of the time, a kind but less energetic caregiver may work out perfectly. Once the child starts to throw a ball, ride a bike, and generally be more active, Janice prefers a more active caregiver.

"This isn't necessarily an age issue. I've had some very lazy younger babysitters. I am more interested in the person's mentality. What do they think a caregiver should do with the child?"

Once her child is in junior high school, Fuchs intends to hire more of a disciplinarian than a playmate, "someone who says to my son, 'It's time to do your chores and finish your homework.'"

Recognizing that their children were constantly changing is the reason Tom and Ruth Harkin implemented the nanny-of-the-year program. "We hired a new person to come live with us every year for two reasons: We wanted to be the dominant adults in our children's lives, and we wanted to keep them stimulated."

They recruited young women who were very stimulating but also who needed to be stimulated. "That's why we kept them only one year. These were women who just finished college and were in the exploratory stages of their lives. They wanted to live in the comfort and safety of a home but in a new geographic location," says Ruth.

The Harkins felt there was a high burnout rate that comes with being a nanny. So each year they looked for a person who filled the needs of the family in that particular year. "One year we would concentrate on the girls learning a language, so our nanny would be bilingual. Another year we concentrated on sports."

There were years they had nannies they hated to see leave, so some stayed a little longer. But they usually discovered they were right in choosing a one-year time limit. "Young people grow out of experiences fast!"

The Harkins' nanny-of-the-year program proves just how creative working parents can be to enlist not only good help but to enhance their children's lives in their absence.

Judith Regan introduces talented people into her children's lives, too. "I met this great guy who builds boats with my son. It's important to create an extended family, especially when you are a single mom."

THE ENDLESS LIST

Maybe we have been blessed with husbands who turned out to be terrific dads. And maybe our children are learning how to become team players who consistently cooperate (see

Chapter 4). Perhaps we've finally found the answer to a working mother's prayer: the perfect nanny or house keeper. Free at last! Right?

Perhaps not. Janice Fuchs says we must understand that men and women think differently. She made her point by telling me the "Endless List" story when I interviewed her at her office in Newport Beach, California. "A therapist had a husband and wife put together all the things that they are responsible for in the area of parenting. The husband put down 50 wonderful things, and the wife put down 600 mundane things from the birthday party invitations, to the doctors' appointments, to the dental hygienist visits. For us mothers, it is an *endless list*. Although our husbands may be wonderful about going grocery shopping or completing a list of errands we compiled, we still have this computer chip in our head that says we are responsible for everything."

She's right. I feel responsible that we have the right theme for the birthday party and every child has a favor and the games are right. And I spend $6 a minute calling Kathleen from 35,000 feet up in the air to remind her not to miss her orthodontist's appointment. And will she have her homework turned in on time?

I seem to need to do this in spite of the fact that I am married to a true dude and a willing partner. Yes, he is a very active participant, but I still feel the ultimate responsibility.

Janice thinks in some ways it's an asset.

"I can be in the middle of a business meeting when I suddenly think, *I can't forget to pack the galoshes for my son when we go to Maine in May because it will be raining.* Out of the blue, I'll write myself sticky notes reminding myself to buy character underwear. This is all happening in the midst of negotiating a million-dollar lease with Bloomingdales. That is what makes me successful. I can manage the multitask orientation of what we do and being flexible to boot."

The moral of this story? If you want to keep bringing home and frying that bacon, ladies, go right ahead. But shame on you for singing those "free the slave" blues.

CHAPTER FOUR

Being Responsible

Mother Teresa's words define my life: "We are called upon not to be successful, but faithful."

To me, being faithful implies remaining devoted to my responsibilities. They are obligations that can only be fulfilled by performing certain acts day in and day out. These acts, over time, then become my routines. When I faithfully and lovingly execute them, they lead me to the fulfillment of my vocation.

Balancing motherhood and a career is not a vocation to be taken lightly. The scope and implications of this multifaceted calling are so vast that achieving our true purpose requires the self-discipline of an athlete. I asked working mom and four-time Olympic high diving gold medalist Pat McCormick what this dual vocation and her Olympic training had in common.

"First, a deep sense of responsibility regarding one's commitments; and second, the focus to carry these commitments out. It's one thing to say you are responsible for carrying out your goal, but it is another thing to prove it. I proved I could do it by establishing a routine and focusing on it. Every day at a certain time, I climbed up to the highest step on the diving board and plunged into the pool.

"Later on, when I became a mother, I tapped into my ability to focus again. I knew that if I wanted to spend time with my children and go to school to better myself, I would have to get into the routine of rising at 3:00 A.M. This allowed me to carry out certain other routines with my children later in the day."

Focus with the passion of a gold medalist.

Pat is quick to point out that the routine of getting up in the middle of the night to study may not be appropriate for everyone. For someone else, it might be not receiving phone calls and switching on her answering machine at a certain time every day in order to study. Pat's method could turn another mother hostile and ineffective for the rest of the day. Every mother looks at her unique situation, tests out various routines, and then establishes one. The important point is that, once she has established a routine, she sticks faithfully to it.

Two words, *responsibility* and *focus*, create a happy family life. I know firsthand that it is impossible to discover happiness if I don't act responsibly. Every mother who contributed to this book ended up becoming faithful to her responsibilities. Being responsible is how we discovered our personalized path to happiness.

For example, if you set a goal to graduate from college, it is the routine of attending classes over the next four years that will make that achievement possible. It is that simple. We humans are the ones who make goal attainment so complex. We take side trips, allowing ourselves to get lazy, and then we give in to our desire for instant gratification. Or we allow ourselves to become distracted and interrupted. Or, as Pat McCormick warns, we may force ourselves to try to attain the goal using someone else's routine, which may not be compatible with our situation or personality.

However, what clearly defines any calm working mother is her dedication to several types of routines. We invent our own routines, but we leave plenty of room for flexibility. So, take heed, working mothers: Routine is the peaceful solution to your multifaceted life. Take comfort in it.

When I met Holly (not her real name), she was a single mother with two children under six. She was in charge of the bakery department at my local grocery store. As I wrote this book, I couldn't decide if Holly belonged in this chapter or the one about overcoming obstacles. She definitely qualifies for both, but what impressed me most was her faithfulness and committed self-discipline to a daily routine that ultimately allowed her to accomplish her goals.

Delay gratification for more lasting satisfactions.

She was one of twelve kids. When Holly was growing up, her diabetic mother was always sick and stayed in bed all day. Holly cannot remember her mom ever making a bed or preparing dinner.

Holly's goal was to grow up and have plenty of energy and never be sick all the time like her mother was. She wanted to become both a mom and a baker. Growing up, she baked great cakes and cookies for her brothers and sisters. This was a trade with great earning potential that she felt she could take anywhere.

She married and got pregnant right out of high school. After the baby was born, she took a job as a sandwich maker in the deli of the local grocery store, earning $4 an hour. Her husband was unemployed, so every day he drove the baby to the store at Holly's break time so she could nurse the baby in the car.

By the time they had two children they divorced, and she was left to pay off thousands of dollars of her ex's credit card debt. She was also 100 pounds overweight.

"But I had achieved my goals: I was a mother, and the store had just promoted me to baker. So it became a question of me acting responsibly to fulfill my commitments.

The nature of my job and the hours required made some people think it would be impossible for me to lose the weight and raise my children. But the three of us stuck to our little routines."

Here's what those "little" routines were: At 3:00 A.M. every morning, she gently carried her two sleeping toddlers from their beds to her car. When she got to her babysitter's house down the block, she transferred the girls, without disturbing their sleep, to her sitter's living room couch. There they slept soundly until daylight.

By 8:00 A.M. (this was considered her lunch break), she was back at the sitter's house to take one child to kindercare. With forty-five minutes to spare before returning to the bakery, she went for her daily run through the park. By 12:30 P.M. she picked up the kids, "and we were together for the rest of the day."

Good health is your first priority.

Holly followed this routine for three years, losing 100 pounds in the process. The last time I talked to her, she was the head of the bakery department.

What was the real secret to the fulfillment of her responsibilities?

"The more weight I lost, the more energy I gained. Without energy, it would have become impossible to carry out the rest of my routines."

Your Number-One Priority

You must make your physical routine a priority before you implement any other advice from this book. See a doctor for a checkup first.

Holly's life would have turned into a disaster if she hadn't made her fitness routine one of her number-one priorities.

Kathy Smith says what you accomplish throughout the day depends on your energy level and overall health. Forget buying expensive time planners and learning strategies to better manage your day if you are physically exhausted and susceptible to every germ in the air.

Your responsibilities as mother, wife, and worker can only be performed at high energy levels if you feel good. And when we moms have plenty of energy, we are unstoppable.

> **Movement creates energy.**

"I talk to mothers constantly who complain they have no energy. They are in their forties. They are finally taking a look at their health, and it's not a pretty picture. They say they have no time to exercise. No time for even a walk?" says Kathy Smith.

When she consults with these women who say they have no time to exercise, the first thing she does is take a look at their day. She asks them to write a schedule.

"This is when I get tough and tell them if they don't have time to take care of themselves, something is radically wrong with their lifestyle. They must reevaluate."

She says it takes guts to get off the routine of saying, "This is the way it is, and it won't change, even if I get sick and die." Any time Kathy gets sick, she asks herself what is going on in her life that is causing her to push too hard. What needs to change?

"To have a healthy lifestyle allows you to be a wonderful mom, but most important, a happy person."

Another fitness advocate is Kathie Davis, who is head of IDEA: The Health & Fitness Source. Its mission is good health for everyone. I asked Kathie and the people at IDEA if they would come up with a simple fitness/nutrition program for working mothers. Know in advance that this is a long-term investment in both your own and your family's future welfare.

The Working Mothers' Exercise Plan for Achieving High Energy

How to Begin Your Exercise Program

1. **Plan Exercise into Your Day**

Follow the working mothers' exercise and get-real fitness program.

What if you don't have time to exercise? This is the most common reason most mothers give for not exercising. Before we go on, stop and think a moment. You can make time for anything you are committed to doing. Before you had your children, you were terrified you wouldn't be able to fit them into your schedule. Not surprisingly, you make time. Why? Because you are committed to having children in your life. Similarly, you can become committed to exercise. Relax. It won't take as much time as your children, but they will be forever grateful to you that you cared enough about them to exercise.

Look at your schedule. Take a calendar or PDA that lists the hours of every day in the week. Then fill in what activities you have to do in every hour. (If you can't do this from memory, try making a log for one week.) Notice where you have blank spots, even if they are just for half an hour. Could you fit a short five- to ten-minute walk into that slot?

Make an appointment to exercise. Identify various times you have available, and make appointments with yourself to exercise at those times. Actually write the appointments into your daily planner.

2. **Set Up a Support Network**

Develop a support network consisting of two sets of people. In the first set, include people who will exercise with you. Can you enlist the aid of neighbors, family members, or friends at work? Let your enthusiasm motivate these people. Position exercise as a great adventure you are embarking on.

In the second set, include people who will support you in your efforts.

They might not exercise with you, but they will encourage you through the pitfalls. Do you know any people who are already consistent exercisers? Enlist their aid. They will usually be happy to encourage you to exercise because they are already sold on its benefits.

What about the people who will try to sabotage you? Explain to them that you are trying to develop healthy habits and that exercise is important to you. Ask them to join you and tell them that you'd appreciate their support. Even if they won't support you, they'll be more aware of your needs and hopefully won't sabotage you to such a great extent.

3. **Set Goals**

Why do you want to exercise? To lose weight, build muscle, improve your health, and increase your energy level? If you write down specific goals, you will know what direction to go in. With each of my pregnancies, I gained 50 pounds and I was resembling a full-blown blimp after those babies popped out.

I came up with a great way to motivate myself. I did it right after I saw Jane Fonda in *On Golden Pond*. In one scene she dove off the pier into a lake wearing a bikini. I can remember all of us women in the movie theater gasping out loud. Jane was forty years old at the time, but her body looked twenty-five.

A few days later, I cut out a picture of her in that scene that was published in *People* magazine. I taped it to my refrigerator. Every day, when I'd be tempted to go for the mocha almond fudge ice cream, Jane would give me the evil eye.

The other motivational strategy I used was trying on my pre-pregnancy blue jeans, the jeans I bought when I was exactly the weight that I now wanted to be again. I squeezed into them the first thing in the morning.

If you do this, prepare to be temporarily depressed. I couldn't get the jeans up over my big, fat you-know-what. Then I would go out and do my morning run. Believe me, that routine will keep your legs in motion.

Day by day, week by week, I was able to inch them closer to my waist. It took about nine months (the amount of time it took to put on the weight). Then came the day I could zip up and button, and strut around the house saying to myself, "Eat your heart out, Jane Fonda."

Originally, my goal for achieving my ideal weight was to look good, but after following a lifetime regimen of exercise, I do it now for the mental and spiritual benefits. I am just plain ornery if I do not exercise regularly.

- Make goals that you can chart because then you can see progress toward them.

- Create a short-term plan for next month and then one for a longer period of time, say for four or six months.

- Set realistic goals, for example, walking five more minutes every week, or losing one pound of fat a month. Don't expect to lose thirty pounds in two weeks. (If you are a new mom and you are nursing, you won't lose that last five pounds until you wean the baby, so relax and enjoy your bonding experience. The rest will come off in due time.)

- As motivation, set a target date for accomplishing your goals.

For optimal physical fitness, you'll want to work up to performing cardiovascular exercise like walking or bicycling three to five times per week for twenty to sixty minutes. Of course, whatever exercise you do will provide health gains so don't worry if you can't reach this frequency at first.

If setting goals sounds challenging, do not despair. Enlist the aid of an experienced exerciser, personal trainer, or fitness instructor to help you. Next comes the tough part.

How to Stick with Exercise

Identify potential reasons why you would skip exercise. Write these excuses down. Brainstorm ways you can work around obstacles. For example, how do you fit exercise into the lunch hour? You could bring lunch from home, go for a walk, then eat at your desk, or you could go for a walk and stop by a deli on the way back from your walk.

Find a role model. Enlist mom and fitness guru Kathy Smith as your new role model. She truly walks the talk of good health. Here are some fitness tips from your new mentor:

EAT LIGHTLY THROUGHOUT THE DAY

"Women should take goody bags to the office. Then you will have the right things to eat and won't be at the mercy of vending machines at 3:00 in the afternoon. Mindlessly reaching for a chocolate bar at that time of day will give you a fast energy boost but an immediate letdown. Fresh fruit snacks are so much better with a few slices of turkey for a protein hit."

Eating healthy food creates energy.

SCHEDULE THIRTY MINUTES OF EXERCISE DAILY

This takes discipline, but calm working mothers have it. Remember what Patti McCord told us? She is in the office every morning at 5:30 A.M. to meet her coworker and running partner. They run several miles and then come back to the office and shower and dress before the rest of the staff arrives. "It's tough getting out of bed at that hour when it is dark out in January or February, but it has to become a mindless routine."

By 7:00 A.M., she feels like a million dollars. I can relate. The first ten minutes of my run are sometimes really tough. I keep telling myself to turn around and head home. But I have learned to pay no attention to my weakest thoughts. Just keep going.

Kathy Smith says, "Working mothers say to me that they have to get up at 5:30 A.M. in order to get their children to day care by 7:00 to be at work on time. They claim they simply do not have time to exercise. So here's what I suggest.

"How about twice a week asking your husband to pop the casserole (which you made and froze earlier in the week) into the oven and make the salad while the children set the table. Then take thirty minutes and turn on an exercise video or do your stationary bike. Or how about when the nice weather begins, an after-dinner walk with the family and the dog?"

Kathy Smith is able to find time in the busiest people's day for thirty minutes of exercise. "What about using the lunch break for a thirty minute walk? Have something light two or three days a week and get together with other gals at the office and speed walk around town."

Kathy says if you have prepared your food ahead of time and only heating is required, then, when you get home from work, instead of food preparation, you can go out and play soccer or basketball in the driveway with the kids.

WEAR A PORTABLE STEREO IF YOU WORK OUT ALONE

You will find that your favorite music or a novel on tape will help keep your interest and motivate you to keep going.

SET YOUR EXERCISE BAG BY THE FRONT DOOR THE NIGHT BEFORE YOU WANT TO EXERCISE

This way, you won't forget to take it to work. Going directly from work to exercise is one way of making sure you get there.

MAKE APPOINTMENTS TO EXERCISE WITH A FRIEND

This will motivate you to exercise, because you will want to see your friend. Also, you will be less likely to cancel, because you won't want to let your friend down. Caution: Pick a committed friend who is in the same time zone as you, meaning if you are a morning person and go running with a night person, they will be either late or not show up more times than they will meet you. This happened to me at one point. Then, when she didn't show, I found it a great excuse to go get a cappuccino and muffin instead. My rationale was, "Maybe we can get together later."

TRY A VARIETY OF PROGRAMS TO AVOID BOREDOM

Cross-training is the name of the game. Potential activities include walking, running, swimming, working out on cardiovascular equipment, strength training, hiking, and aerobic dance. Exercise is a family affair at our house. All my daughters are great dancers and aerobicizers. By the time each of them was in the sixth grade, not only were they taking normal dance classes with other kids their age, but they also attended aerobics classes with me at the gym.

My husband and I love to hike. We live in the Sawtooth Mountains in Idaho. Once a week in the summer we climb to the top of our great ski mountain, Mount Bald. Besides hiking other beautiful trails, we in-line skate, downhill ski, snowshoe, and ice skate. The added spiritual benefits of communing with nature help us maintain our attitude of gratitude.

Kathie Davis schedules exercise for seven days a week and keeps it exciting because she diversifies. "Some days I play tennis, handball, or basketball with the kids. Combining my fitness time with family time keeps us together and having fun but also instills a love of fitness in my children. The earlier they get involved in fitness, the easier it will be as they get older to stick to it as part of the way they live."

DON'T PUSH YOURSELF TOO HARD WHEN YOU EXERCISE

You will receive little additional benefit from exercising out of your comfort zone. Exercise should be a little bit of a challenge, but if it is too difficult, you won't want to continue.

SET UP A REWARD SYSTEM FOR YOURSELF

Promise yourself that if you exercise for a given number of days, you will give yourself something that you want. This may be time for yourself, a weekend trip, a new CD, or something else that you'd like.

KEEP A LOG OF THE TIMES YOU'VE EXERCISED

This visual reminder of your accomplishments will make you feel good about already having exercised so many times. It will help motivate you to continue.

SEEK OUT INFORMATION ON HEALTH AND ILLNESS

The more knowledgeable you become, the better able you'll be to guide your program. Try reading books and magazines or talking to fitness instructors or personal trainers.

USE AFFIRMATIONS

Affirmations make it easier to establish new habits by programming your subconscious to accept new beliefs. They should be positive statements and start with words like "I am" or "I have." For example, one might be, "I am living a healthy lifestyle by walking twice a week at lunch."

Repeat affirmations several times a week. You might feel that saying affirmations is lying to yourself if you haven't already achieved the goal, but that's okay. As long as the statement is a believable and achievable goal, this is fine.

What to Expect When You Start a Program

Exercise should not be dangerous if you start out gradually and build up to more strenuous activities. It's a good idea to check with your doctor before starting an exercise program. This is true especially if you have a prior history of injuries or medical conditions (including high blood pressure or high cholesterol), are pregnant, smoke cigarettes, have a family history of heart disease, or you are a woman over fifty.

Beginner exercisers must start slow and build.

You might feel stiff or sore when you first start a program, but you should *never* feel pain. Pain is your body's way of telling you that something is wrong. You also shouldn't feel exhausted at the end of a workout.

If you feel pain or feel yourself getting overtired or out of breath, you should check with your doctor. Muscle soreness tells you that exercise is affecting your body, so it is actually a good sign. Don't worry, however, because the soreness will last only a few days.

On the following page is an exercise planning worksheet Kathie Davis of IDEA: The Health & Fitness Source recommends you use if you are a newcomer to this business of exercising.

HEALTHY EATING ROUTINES

Daniel Kosich, Ph.D., is the contributing editor for IDEA Publications. He is also the author of a simple and speedy guide to weight management, a book entitled *Get Real*.

Planning Worksheet

Times of the day I've identified when I can exercise:
Time #1 _____
Time #2 _____
Time #3 _____

Days that are good for me to work out:
Day #1 _____
Day #2 _____
Day #3 _____

People I like to work out with:
Person #1 _____
Person #2 _____
Person #3 _____

Activities I'd like to try:
Activity #1 _____
Activity #2 _____
Activity #3 _____

Exercise goals I have:
Goal #1 _____
Goal #2 _____
Goal #3 _____

People who will support me in exercise:
Support Person #1 _____
Support Person #2 _____
Support Person #3 _____

Target date to exercise: _____

(Reprinted with permission by IDEA: The Health & Fitness Source 800-999-IDEA, ext. 7)

We mothers do not have time to fool around looking at charts and tables that give us the grams of this or that and then have to calculate all that stuff. We want a no-brainer routine to maintain our ideal weight.

Here's what Daniel suggests in *Get Real:*

EIGHTY/TWENTY AND THE PYRAMID

The U.S. Department of Agriculture recently spearheaded a major project to make it easier for the public to know what they should be eating. The result is the Food Guide Pyramid.

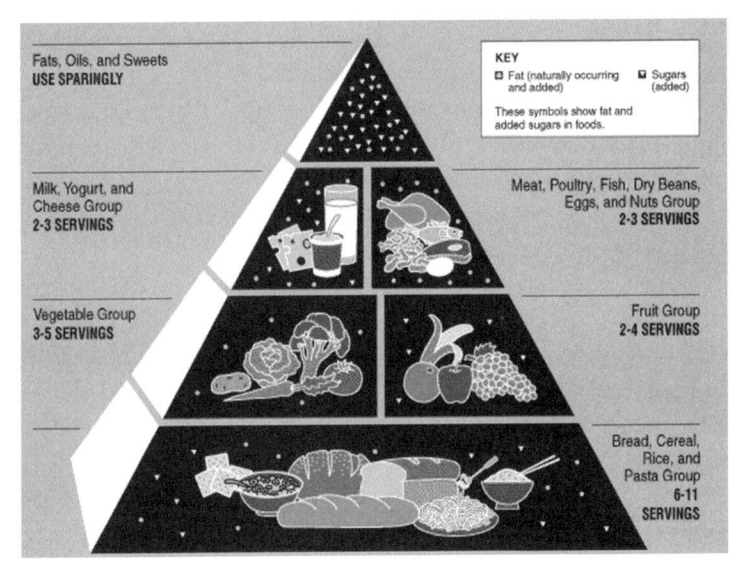

```
Fats, Oils, and Sweets
USE SPARINGLY

KEY
□ Fat (naturally occurring and added)    ■ Sugars (added)
These symbols show fat and added sugars in foods.

Milk, Yogurt, and Cheese Group
2-3 SERVINGS

Meat, Poultry, Fish, Dry Beans, Eggs, and Nuts Group
2-3 SERVINGS

Vegetable Group
3-5 SERVINGS

Fruit Group
2-4 SERVINGS

Bread, Cereal, Rice, and Pasta Group
6-11 SERVINGS
```

"Look at the pyramid and then remember that a sensible daily diet is one that at least 80 percent of the time provides six to eleven servings from the bread, cereal, rice, and pasta group; three to five servings from the vegetable group; two to four servings from the fruit group; two to three servings from the milk, yogurt, and cheese group; two to three servings from the meat, poultry, fish, dry beans, eggs, and nuts group; and not very much from the fats and sweets group.

"If you don't match these daily servings 20 percent of the time or less, I personally don't think it's that big of a deal. The eighty/twenty approach to using the pyramid is a lifestyle. Hopefully, you can use it for the rest of your life. It means that if you want to go to a Sunday morning buffet brunch, do it. And don't feel guilty about it," says Daniel Kosich.

Keep in mind that everybody's metabolism is different. Some of the current weight-loss books are claiming we have to reduce the amount of carbohydrates (breads, pastas, rice) that we eat and increase the protein amounts. I gauge carbohydrates versus protein intake on the amount of aerobic exercise I do. Ten years ago, I was both teaching and taking high-impact aerobics classes almost daily. I found I could get away with eating a lot more carbohydrates than I can now.

My age plus the decrease in the amount of time I exercise daily does not justify all that starch in my diet. This is why we all suggest you get a personal trainer to figure out what is best for you, but the eighty/twenty pyramid is a very helpful guide.

There you have it, mothers. If you want to delve into more detail on the subject of weight loss and foods, I highly recommend you pick up Daniel's book or call IDEA: The Health & Fitness Source headquarters (858-535-8979) in San Diego to order it.

You may not need to do all the things I suggested in this section. Some of us have a harder time getting started with certain routines than others, so I wanted to give you plenty of ways to motivate yourself. Pick and choose what is most appropriate for you. The most important thing is to start to move today.

MENTAL ROUTINES

A working mother has to be thinking clearly and rationally at all times. My contributing working moms all had to learn how to be able to shift gears at the last minute without panicking. When a change of plans disrupts our schedule, here is where a calm mind-set pays off.

You make matters worse by fighting the inevitable. Your child has an ear infection or, worse yet, falls off a skateboard and gets a concussion. You are called out of a meeting at work and must rush to the emergency room of some hospital.

I'm not trying to be morbid, but this double-duty life requires you to have your head about you at all times. Over the years, I had to learn how to knock off the dramatics and deal with the situation. If you are not peaceful as you go about your business, you are not only driving yourself nuts, you are not a very good role model for your child.

David Royko, a psychologist and the clinical director of Cook County, Illinois, Marriage and Family Counseling Service, says, "What children need more than anything else, though it might sound glib, is peace . . . a relatively conflict-free set of parents."

You cannot deal with conflict if you personally are not at peace. Complaining doesn't help, either. You have to be willing to think and act responsibly to reduce your stress. You have to be willing to work on yourself mentally the same way as you do physically.

It's always been much harder for me to take responsibility to get fit mentally than it is physically. As hard as it is to stay in good physical shape, I can put on my running shoes. I can hit the pavement and move my legs and arms. By the end of my forty-five-minute run, I can feel the sweat. My cheeks are red. I am thinking clearly.

But with invisible mental exercise routines, it takes more time and patience before the payoffs start rolling into your head. I tend to be impatient. I want it now. So guess what! I am the perfect candidate for meditation. My mind wanders when I meditate.

What finally straightened me out was the realization that I needed a mental fitness coach just like some folks need a physical fitness personal trainer to help dig them out of their own fat and inertia. I needed one to help save me from drowning in the raging waters of my flooded mind.

Meditate. I became a believer once I saw the positive effects meditation has had on some friends of mine who recovered from heart disease. Their doctors recommended regular meditation routines to reduce their stress. Even the American Medical Association advocates it now.

In spite of all the good reports about meditation, I still had to be willing to set aside the time just the way I did for my aerobics class or jogging. The few moments of retreating to silence and turning inward when the tension mounts has made a major difference in my life.

Once I recognized the need, I discovered the writings and tapes of the late Father Anthony DeMello. Before he has you meditating, he teaches you exercises to increase your awareness. Awareness truly is the key that unlocks the door to your self-imposed stress. I needed to become aware of how I was reacting stressfully to certain situations that occurred in my day. DeMello's teachings helped me with such an awareness. I saw firsthand by observing myself during those moments when I was willing to be silent.

Lao-tse says, "Silence is the great revelation."

A wonderful beginner meditation I highly recommend is Kathy Smith's BLT Technique. Remember, you have to discipline yourself and commit to this exercise. Block out all thoughts of skepticism. Such doubts kept me from making progress for a long time.

Kathy Smith's BLT Technique

When you start to feel the pressures of your demanding lifestyle, there are certain things you can do to diminish the stress and gain your perspective. This activity should become part of your daily routine. When I went to Los Angeles to interview Kathy Smith, she said earlier in the day she was feeling stressful. By the time I arrived, she appeared calm, cool, and very collected.

I asked her how she turned her day around.

"Danielle, today was one of those mornings when things were not clicking. Steve is out of town today, so when the family got up, things were slightly different. One of my clients called early—7:45. That made me nervous because the kids had to be at school by 8:30. Plus I am chairing the Multiple Sclerosis Race this weekend. So next someone on the committee called because there was a question about music."

Meanwhile, she was making lunches, and her little one was in a bad mood. Next, she drove the girls to school. "I got this panicky sensation inside. But I have trained myself and learned what I can do to calm down. I paused for a few moments for a BLT." (Breath = Listen Theory)

Breathe and listen.

Stop and learn Kathy's technique right now so the next time all hell breaks loose, you can calm yourself.

"It doesn't matter when the panic sets in. After you let the kids out of the car or if you are at your office, stop whatever you are doing for a few minutes and sit back quietly.

"Inhale for the count of six.

"Hold your breath for the count of six and during the hold, listen to the sounds around you.

"Now exhale. Do it again, and listen a little harder this time. This time, you may pick up children's laughter or the sound of the air conditioning unit in your office along with car noises. Now exhale again."

Kathy suggests you do this, about four times, and each time you will find yourself listening harder and harder. The theory behind this is when you get into these panicky situations—when your mind starts jumping way ahead with "I gotta do this and I gotta do that"—you must focus on reentering mentally into the present moment.

"Once you calm down, you are more capable of solving problems. The other thing I try to remind myself is that problems will always be with me. The problem is not the problem. The problem is my reaction to the problem," says Kathy.

The real problem, then, is the way we cope. This is what destroys us. Not the problem.

"The BLT helps you to cope differently. And the bonus is coping differently equals dealing differently with the problems, too."

This is old hat for Ginna Bragg, who started practicing meditation when she was a young working mother of twenty-five.

"I meditate before I even get out of bed in the morning. Whether it is concentrating on my breathing or using a mantra (a sound you utter and concentrate on), meditation is always about staying both physically and mentally in the present moment. You can find ways of meditating while sitting in front of the school waiting for your child to be dismissed or while waiting in the dentist's or doctor's office."

Ginna believes meditation is a must for every mother. She has seen firsthand how learning meditation can transform lives.

"Frenzied working mothers who come to learn how to meditate with Deepak Chopra at his center, where I work, leave much calmer and happier. They take home a tool that helps keep them peaceful and in the present moment."

Yoga is another great way to practice meditation and get in shape. My yoga instructor, Richard Odom, at the Sun Valley Athletic Club, teaches a meditation and breathing exercise I now practice regularly.

You can literally do this meditation anywhere, too. Get in a comfortable position and begin concentrating on your breathing. As you inhale, silently say to yourself, "My body is strong." As you exhale, silently say to yourself, "My mind is at peace."

I love that one. Often I say and breathe it sitting at my desk or while flying on an airplane. I've trained myself to calm down within minutes of its recitation.

Sharon D'Orsie practices what "the Italians do every afternoon; she takes a nap. At age forty-eight, I bought myself a terrific birthday present: a couch for my office. When things get too crazy, I take either a twenty minute nap or meditate while lying down. I go back to my desk thoroughly refreshed. It really has helped my productivity."

Family Routines

I really believe children want and deserve continuity in their lives. Adults aren't any different. I find joy and comfort in my daily routine of running two miles to church before attending Mass and sitting peacefully in the pew waiting for the priest as the sun streams through the stained-glass windows. Or sipping my cappuccino while reading the morning newspaper at my favorite local coffee shop. Or putting clean sheets on the bed every Saturday morning.

My son Daniel still loves "mush." It's a cheap hamburger dish made with ground beef, tomato soup, and canned mixed vegetables poured over mashed potatoes that we used to eat every Tuesday night when he was growing up. He tells me he finds comfort in making that dish for himself whenever he's had an especially stressful Tuesday.

The Best of Both Worlds Routine

Instead of thinking your family and career life are in conflict with one another, start realizing each life equalizes the other one. Most of us working mothers are the type that have a lot of energy and get bored easily, anyway. We enjoy variety in our life. The routine of being able to dance back and forth between our professional and personal worlds can actually be a way to reduce stress.

"When I have been loaded down with work and stress on my job with seemingly no end in sight, I take the pause that refreshes. Then I tell my staff I am going home for the rest of the day to concentrate on another phase of my life," says Ruth Harkin.

"Working mothers have so many phases of their life to explore. And leaving one phase to go explore another is truly a great stress reliever."

Kelly Radaker Jones enjoys the best of both worlds routine for the same reason.

"Being able to have both, one enhances the other. When I am home for a while and not traveling on business trips, and it is mid-afternoon and the kids have been fighting all day, I appreciate my work and look forward to the following week's business trip. Then, when I go out on the trip and I am struggling to complete a project with my clients who are being especially difficult, I can't wait to get home to my babies."

Realize you have the best of both worlds. Live in the present moment when you are on the job, and make the most of it. Then, when you've had enough, close the door of your office (both physically and mentally) and enter the door of your home (both physically and mentally) and enjoy the present moment while you are there. Don't be like some working mothers who are never where they are supposed to be. Sure, it may appear they are at the office because they are there physically, but they are worried about what is going on at home. The opposite is also true. This makes for unproductive living. No one around you ever gets the honor of your presence.

The Ideal-Scene Blueprint/Schedule Routine

Begin the day with either a written or mental blueprint of how this day would go if everything fell into place, with no emergencies, changes of plans, etc. Here's how this either plays out in your head or on paper:

Today is Wednesday, which means the girls have choir practice after school. I must accomplish all my _____ by 3:00.

Due to an early morning advertising meeting, I have to shift my running time to noon.

No lunch appointments today. Eat a light lunch at my desk after the run.

Devote two hours to uninterrupted writing/projects.

Let voice mail pick up messages for two hours.

Remind babysitter/brother/sister/husband to pick up girls after choir practice.

Meet family at home at 6:00 for dinner, which either I or ? has arranged to prepare or bring to the house.

Answer all personal correspondence after the children go to bed.

Call the airport to see if the last flight came in so I can determine whether I need to allow extra time in the morning to catch my plane out of town.

The ideal-scene blueprint is referred to merely as "the schedule" at the Harkin household. Senator Tom Harkin told me, "The one thing Ruth has done our entire married life, and she holds my feet to the fire on it, is to make a schedule. We have a year schedule. Yep. The whole year is written out. So we know when our family is going to where and when.

August 3 to 8, Congress break, so we all go to Hawaii; September 10, drive our daughter to college.

"Then, when people call us up, we aren't fibbing when we say no. The schedule goes to our staff, and they say to the caller that Senator Harkin or Ruth is already scheduled."

Tom says you have to stick to the schedule as best you can. "You simply cannot run this family/career operation by the seat of your pants. Plus you cannot say, 'I will do all these other things, and then, when I get time, I will get to my family!' If you do, your personal relationships with your spouse and children will go to hell."

Prevent problems by spotting critical paths.

Sharon D'Orsie is highly organized and relies on her schedule, too. She says that the schedule helps her identify "the critical-path items connected with the execution of all projects, both personal and professional."

The critical-path items are the potential problems or bottlenecks. "Say I am supposed to do a job in New Orleans during Mardi Gras. I have, sitting in front of me, the following year's schedule. I look at it, knowing there are several critical-path items I must deal with. I am very good at spotting critical-path items. I realize because it will be Mardi Gras week, the biggest critical-path item is getting a place to sleep. Why figure out how to get there or what equipment I must bring if I cannot find a place to sleep or shower?

"I solve that problem and then spot the next critical-path item: the kids will be out of school that exact same week I am in New Orleans due to midwinter break. I will call Grandma and see if she can plan a trip to our house during that week. That would solve that problem."

Sharon points out the other good thing about the schedule and being able to spot critical-path items is that you identify children's activities and events that are crucial to attend. Because this is done way ahead of time, you plan to go to the event. If you cannot, you have time to discuss this with the children and delegate a grandparent, aunt, or cherished friend to attend the event. This is all discussed way in advance with the child.

"As long as you are there for at least half of the big deals, and for the other half, they have someone cheering them in the audience, they really do not get upset when you are not there."

If you travel in your work like I do, it is critical to get your hands on the school calendar the first week of school in September so you can sit down and go over all the important events with your child. Dates such as school open houses, Christmas pageants, and parent conferences need to be written in permanent ink on your calendars. Get agreement on what you cannot or can participate in right up front. I prevented a lot of disappointment and heartache on the home front using this routine.

The Shifting Gears Routine

Here's the challenge. Something could come up and completely cancel the ideal-scene blueprint. This is tricky because you have to be able to move through your day following a certain vision but at the same time be focused very carefully on the present moment and be ready at the drop of a hat to shift gears. Be careful of what you allow to change your plans.

You learn to sacrifice anything unnecessary that messes up your family routine. Janice Fuchs purposely doesn't have manicures right now because it takes too much time away from her children and would stop certain regular family routines. Her husband doesn't play golf on Saturday for the same reason.

So you change your plans, remaining flexible for the sake of the family or some important business circumstances. For example, Shirley Pepys says, "When my children were very little, I learned to make decisions minute by minute. Every minute of each new day I was weighing my children's agendas alongside my business commitments.

"One day I might say to myself that I need to take Tiffany to her ice skating lessons, so I will shift gears and visit the buyer at Sears tomorrow."

Be prepared at all times.

But she had to be thinking clearly, because what if the store buyer wouldn't be in the next day? Shirley knows she has to have a list of names of other skating mothers on hand who she could call on to get Tiffany a ride to the rink in case today is the only day the buyer will be in this week. Other options? Dad might leave work early and drive her. Or perhaps Tiffany was old enough to get on the bus and go herself.

If you become rigid or inflexible, the double life is going to drive you nuts. You must remain open to change to make your life work. Remember what we said about having the best of both worlds.

Look at it this way: With family and work commitments, nothing is ever dull. There is always a surprise around the corner. Some people have to go to the movies to seek thrills and get their adrenaline going. But with us, all we have to do is wake up in the morning and the old adrenaline will rise and fall enough throughout our day to keep us on the edge of our seats and on our toes.

The Night-Before Routine

Debbie Sarnowski says, "I am not a morning person, so our routines have to be done in the evenings before bedtime. Night routines make my mornings tolerable. My children had routine chores to do before bedtime since they have been very young. They lay their clothes out before bedtime. This includes their shoes. Have you ever panicked in the morning looking for a kid's shoe? This mishap sets the mood for the entire family for the rest of the day."

Sharon D'Orsie solved the one-shoe-lost problem by making her daughter Laura go to school once with two different shoes. "Funny thing, but after that, Laura could always find her shoes. This is the kind of stuff I do not tolerate because it causes so much stress in a household."

Debbie Sarnowski's entire home functions smoothly 80 percent of the time because of before-bedtime routines.

"They pick up toys. Wash the chairs in the kitchen after dinner. Set the table for tomorrow's breakfast. Two of my children take their baths at night and two in the morning. They all know how to make their own cereal. The older ones help the younger ones."

The Saturday Morning Routine

Debbie has another routine she touts. "It's called Saturday Morning Cleanup. The kids get up at eight, and I make a nice big breakfast. Then everybody has a chore to do. The older kids clean the baseboards. Then the windows and mirrors are cleaned. The furniture is dusted. Divide the work and conquer the job."

Widowed working mother Joan Kershner believed in the Saturday morning work routine, too, but added fun as a bonus on every Saturday afternoon. Through the years she says they drank chocolate sodas, jumped on trampolines, rode horses, went on picnics, sailed, and golfed once all the chores were completed.

Including play and fun times in the routine has carried over into the adult relationships Joan has with her children. They still get together frequently, just like lifelong friends do, because of those early childhood routines and experiences.

The Airplane Routine

I, too, have established certain routines so that when my children were out of school or my husband came home, I did not find myself doing work that I could have done when they were in school, sleeping, or with their friends. For example, I do a lot of writing and paperwork while traveling on airplanes. This, too, has required discipline because I've had to fight the tendency to want to watch the movie, eat the meal, read magazines, or just sleep.

It feels so good when I stick to my routine while flying. That routine involves bringing my laptop computer and turning it on as soon as the stewardess gives us the go-ahead to use it.

I am a happy camper and very satisfied with myself when I return home from a trip and know that I don't have to tell my family I cannot go to the movies with them or turn down the opportunity to chaperon a field trip because I am behind in my work.

The Car Phone Routine

Janice Fuchs uses her car phone on the way to work. "I'm in the car forty minutes every morning, so I use that time to make the kids' doctor and dentist appointments, talk to teachers if necessary, and make business calls. That way, when I arrive at the office, I am ready to go for the day." Be careful, however. Accidents increase if you don't pay attention.

Avoiding the Last-Minute Panic Routine

Sharon D'Orsie says this only works when the kids get to be school age. "You make a pact with your children that if they need supplies for a special research project or a purple cape for the play or six dozen cookies, you will be glad to work with them as long as they tell you ahead of time. No last-minute requests. This routine of having them tell you far in advance and you being prepared takes tons of stress off you and teaches them how to get organized early in life."

The One Calendar Fits All Routine

Kathie Davis tried keeping a calendar at the office and at her house. "I stay organized by taking my time planner with me everywhere I go. Every part of my life is written on it. The family commitments, work, exercise. This could also be your ideal-scene blueprint."

The Rock-a-Bye Baby Routine

Many working mothers have a hard time leaving their jobs back at the office or store once they get home. One woman told me she was a nervous wreck when she walked in the door. "I wanted to run into my home office and finish making calls and take out my paperwork, but the kids pounced on me as soon as I walked in the door. I wanted to hold my baby, prepare a meal, and finish a report all at the same time."

She found a way to calm herself down by sitting in a rocker with the baby for the first fifteen minutes after she arrived home. "Just holding the baby and rocking her calmed me down."

The After-Bedtime Routine

Mollie Hunter, a computer sales manager, was always very organized until her two children and three stepchildren came along. Like our rocking chair mom, her biggest problem was shifting gears from work to family when she got home at night. But she is required to do some homework at night, so she can't just come home and rock the baby and forget about the homework.

The only way she can keep her sanity is to put everything aside regarding her job until after the children go to sleep. They are still little, so they are in bed by 7:45 P.M.

Fifteen Minutes in My Room Routine

There is nothing worse than coming home from work only to open the front door and find people waving papers under your nose and yelling, "Sign here or I won't be promoted to the fifth grade." I hate being pounced on at the end of the day. After living through some of this bedlam, I called a family meeting with my brood.

"Do me a favor. When I walk in the door, please repeat the following greeting: 'Good evening, Mother. It's wonderful to have you home again.'"

I in turn, would reply: "And it's wonderful seeing all of you, my little darlings. After I retire to my room to take a refreshing shower, shall we all meet in the kitchen for a friendly family chat?"

By the time your children are in grade school, they can be taught to cut you some slack when you walk in the door. Little babies and toddlers would not understand this routine, but my older children came to respect it. By the time they were teenagers, they were asking me to cut them the same fifteen minutes of slack. Nobody likes to be smothered to death when they get home at night.

The Cook One Day a Month Routine

A friend of mine from Dallas, Texas, got in the routine of cooking nonstop, morning until night, one day a month. When the day was over, she had more than twenty meals in the freezer, ready to go with a bit of heating up in the oven. She was opposed to serving macaroni and cheese or Hamburger Helper and always wanted to put a home-cooked meal on the table. This routine isn't for everybody (like me, for instance).

Thirty Favorite Meals Routine

After a neighbor of mine had her first baby, she became a weekly meal planner. She created a list of her and her husband's favorite thirty dinners. Each week, her husband selected a few from the list and she picked the remaining ones.

She pulls the recipes for each week and does the weekly grocery shopping on Sunday so all the ingredients are available during the week. She leaves the recipes on the refrigerator door with the list of the meals for the week. When her husband gets home from work, he can select the dinner for the evening and begin preparation.

The Ordering-in Routine

One couple I know isn't that big on eating out in restaurants, and they don't like to cook, either. They found a woman who is a gourmet chef. The Thuerbachs choose from her delicious menus the dinners they have a taste for on certain days of the week. She delivers the food and they can either heat it up later or sit down at 5:00 when she brings over the meal. She'll even do the cleanup.

Many restaurants today offer a delivery service that includes all the items on their menus at a reduced rate. On those nights when you have a hankering for Chinese or Italian food from your favorite restaurant but don't have the energy to get in the car, make it easier on yourselves by ordering in. It's always fun to eat dinner in your jammies.

I've never had the guilt that many mothers do about who prepares my food. My husband, the local chefs, and most of my friends are better cooks than I am. I try to sponge a meal off all of these culinary geniuses whenever I get the chance. During the holiday season, I get the urge to cook and bake nonstop. Then I burn myself out for a good part of the rest of the year. So here is my favorite routine.

The Eat Out as Much as Possible Routine

Thanks, moms, for all your great suggestions, but my personal choice is still the eating-out routine. It all started after

I got my freezer. My first goal when I made some money was to buy a freezer. I used to die a thousand deaths at the checkout counter, with children in tow, when the cashier hit the total. I didn't have the money. So the kids were summoned to put half the groceries selected back on the shelves.

It was especially embarrassing watching the dramatics of a nine-year old as he returned the marble fudge ice cream to the freezer department. I died a little every time we had to put stuff back on the shelves. After my first eighteen months of being a successful salesperson, we bought a twenty-two-cubic-foot freezer and filled it with goodies. It was great filling that monster up with food. Then it was even more fun standing around with my family, ogling the food. But, like I told my family the day the freezer was delivered, "It's good to have this food for emergency purposes. However, I never said I'd cook it. So let's just go out to dinner."

If you can afford it, especially during times when your workload is heavy, do what we do at our house—dine out. We have wonderful restaurants in our town.

If we've been working in our home offices all day long, it's a treat to have a change of scenery, and we don't have to do the cleanup after the meal. We justify eating out frequently because we don't have to rent office space to run our home-based business. I have found that I spend more money than I should when I go grocery shopping. Unless I am sure I will have time to cook for a week straight, it is actually cheaper for us to eat out.

Having a Sense of Humor Routine

Are you having fun yet, or are you still acting like Oscar the Grouch? You have to be a little crazy and willing to belly-laugh with the rest of the brood at least once a day. If you want a good roar, try one of the emergency routines I used when I had five babies in seven years.

After one especially harrowing morning of making lunches and searching for lost car keys and homework, I decided we should try a new routine the following night to eliminate all this madness. Everybody, including myself, took a shower and got completely dressed right before bedtime.

"Forget this laying out our school and work clothes routine. Let's just get it over with now and go to bed dressed for tomorrow and be ready when we wake up."

My family thought I had lost it, but we all jumped into my giant, king-size bed fully clothed with a bad case of the giggles. Then the giggling grew into hysterics and became an epidemic throughout the house. I don't think we fell asleep until two in the morning, we were laughing so hard. The moral of the story is, the best routine you should practice regularly with those you love is getting into the habit of having plenty of fun.

Party on, Mom.

CHAPTER FIVE

Mothers on Money: The New Rules

Working mothers have to be highly money motivated. We are realists. The alternative—having no money—means staying trapped. We know that money is a ticket to freedom. Without such freedom we pass on a hopeless, lazy legacy to our children, a legacy that includes no education, no opportunities, no life.

So, yes, we want money for us and our family. We know it contains the solution for providing them with the best future possible. In a profile of six single mothers on welfare, a fourteen-year-old boy was begging his mother to study harder for her nurse's aide test. "Her face framed by long, straight hair, Mary Miller looks up with a tentative, almost apologetic expression at her son after he calls her to the kitchen table to study. 'Come on, Ma, you can do it.'"

Her son knows that soon his mother's welfare checks will come to an end, and "he fears she will be cast to the wind."

No child deserves to live in that kind of fear. Every child born in the world deserves financial security.

Go Back to School

First, it takes an education to ultimately improve your family's economic situation as Marissa Cobb Wearer and Debbie

Sarnowski taught us. They rocked the boat. Sure, they were criticized and ridiculed by family and friends, but they found a place to make their dreams come true: Alverno College. They refused to sit around and play "poor me." Learn from their example. They found a school—weekend college—that could accommodate their special needs. There are hundreds of such places all over the world. True, sacrifices were made on everybody's part, but in the big picture, their children will attest to this fact: The sacrifices were worth it.

Go to school to increase your earning power.

QUIT TRYING TO WIN A POPULARITY CONTEST

One of the reasons we don't try harder stems from our fear of not being liked or loved. It is a flaw many of us working moms need to overcome. Candice Copeland Brooks confessed, "I am really a people-pleaser. I looked at my history and realized I do not like conflict. This is a pattern that stems from my childhood. I used to worry about turning people down. They might get angry or disappointed in me. So I would do what they wanted me to do, but I was left with an emotional hangover that plays out as anger and resentment. Once I quit people-pleasing, my life became much more focused."

People-pleasing can lead to domestic abuse, too. It's the reason Marissa and Debbie kept dropping out of school. But they fought back, refusing to give in to their worst fears.

FORGET THE ALL-OR-NOTHING RULE

Besides eliminating our tendency to please people, we have to forget about the all-or-nothing rule, which makes achieving our goals next to impossible. It took me sixteen years of part-time schooling to get my B.A., and four years of night school to get my M.A. in professional writing. All my children attended my graduations. They were all hoarse the next day from shouting, "Go, Mama," as I strutted across the stage to receive my diplomas.

When I first knew I wanted to go back to school, it was difficult for me to accept that I could not throw myself into it full time. I had many children and a job. So I decided not to enroll because I had the all-or-nothing attitude.

The all-or-nothing attitude is a great excuse for giving up. I am glad I researched schools and found a place that could work with my schedule. By working slowly but steadily on my education over the years, I was able to improve my speaking and writing skills. This has put me more in demand and helped me increase my fees. It's also afforded me the luxury of staying at home more with my children. More money buys more time with those you love.

> **Money buys time.**

If I had waited until I could devote my life to nothing but studying, I would be old and gray. In the long run, I would not have spent as much time with my family due to being stuck in the same old job.

You May Be Worth Millions

Flavia Weedn was separated from her husband and struggling to support two children when she formulated a strategy for generating an income.

"How was I going to raise these kids? We needed food. We needed a place to sleep. Then I asked myself what skills I had. What inside of me could I discover and reach into that would help us survive? I did not look outside of myself. I think this is where some women make a mistake."

Most people look to the classifieds for a job, a company, something outside of themselves to pay the bills. But Flavia looked to herself to determine what she was worth.

"I said to myself, 'Okay, I can write. I can paint. So, what can I do with those two things?'"

First, she answered a magazine ad that said, "Do you love to paint? In your spare time you can earn thousands of dollars."

She signed up pronto.

"They sent me some cheap-looking gifts and I was to paint them in the colors they dictated. But I painted my own colors instead. When they asked me to stick with their production line directions, I quit.

"I had a $50 Plymouth station wagon. The lining of the car was ripped and all hanging. I would pile Lisa and Rick in the backseat and go ask junkyards and thrift shop owners where they put the things they couldn't sell. I took those things home. Rick and Lisa thought this was the greatest thing in the world."

She found and bought old wooden rolling pins and violin cases that she could paint. A broken violin case has soul to me. It's filled with all those feelings. How did it get broken? How many people loved it? What music came from it?"

After she finished painting the pieces, she displayed them in her front yard with a For Sale sign.

"People would just drive by and buy them. Then I started selling my things on the street. For a while, that was the only money I had. I found a way."

Put a big price tag on your worth.

From Flavia we learn two lessons: to look within for answers to money problems, to ask ourselves what skills we have inside that we love to do; and to have courage enough to put a valuable price tag on our work. When she made the transition from painting for pleasure to painting for money, it took her a long time to believe that someone would pay her money to own one of her paintings. Here she tells the story of what happened at one of her first art shows at a local mall.

"The greatest obstacle I had to overcome was to rid myself of overwhelming feelings of inferiority concerning my work in the beginning. I remember well my initial feelings at that first art show when I saw all the professionals around me. I kept taking the paintings in and out of the trunk of my car before I finally set up. At the end of the day, one artist whose work I admired said to me, 'Flavia, I hope you keep painting. Your work has a kind of magic because it sings. And that's the ingredient most artists strive for.'

"During the thirty years since that statement, I have worked with many schooled technicians who are very well skilled and yet whose work has no magic. It's been lost somewhere or overshadowed by what they've been taught.

"So, for me being self-taught was a tremendous advantage. I developed my own style and because I was unafraid to let myself be vulnerable, my work had imagination and feeling. I thank God I had courage enough to take a risk in the beginning, and I am reminded of what might have happened if I hadn't taken the paintings out of my car that day by a quote from Oliver Wendell Holmes: 'Alas for those who never sing, but die with their music still in them.'"

NEW ATTITUDE

When we have the same work experience as a man, there is no reason why we should be earning seventy cents for every dollar that a man earns for doing the exact same job. Did you know that is currently the situation in this country?

You can change the rules. A friend of mine who works on the production side of major blockbuster films tells me a certain female Hollywood box office star is helping both herself and other actresses change their pay scales. But she is considered demanding. My friend told me, "She refuses to settle for less. She's earned the right to ask for the same money to do a film that her male counterparts make, and she stands firm. Plus she asks for certain accommodations for her children: extra trailers, tutors, travel expenses. She wants them with her whenever possible. When her name comes up, its always 'Show me the money' time."

Contrast the star's attitude with one welfare mother of four who is also a thirty-six-year-old grandmother. She said, "It was the way I was raised—you have kids and you go on aid—it was just the natural thing to do. And then, after awhile, you realize you ain't ever going anywhere. You're trapped. And then a lot of them get lazy, just living for the welfare."

The difference in circumstances is the result of a difference of attitudes. Don't buy the excuse that there is no way out of poverty. What if I were to tell you that the box office star came from a childhood of poverty herself? She didn't just sit and putter. She went out, got the training, did the work, and got the reputation. And then, along the way, her thinking changed. With this change of mind-set, new behavior emerged. She took action.

Most of the welfare mothers profiled believe that a few hundred dollars a month is a lot of money. This welfare mentality has been passed down to them for generations.

You and I can help our sisters on this planet break the chains of the past that bind them. It starts with the guilt trips we take concerning money. It's time to adopt a new affirmation: "There is nothing wrong with mixing motherhood and money."

Money and motherhood is good.

The root of all evil is not money but poverty, a poverty mentality that squelches all human potential and sends negative messages to our heart and soul that say, "You deserve little or nothing." It's a kill switch that dramatically reduces the motivated activity of our lives. It leads to hopelessness, which can manifest itself through violence, drugs, and depression.

Make no bones about it. We will not settle for less. We know that money is an important priority.

HOP ON THE MOMMY TRACK THAT LEADS TO NOWHERE?

About ten years ago, a book came out stating that women who do not choose to play the game will never achieve their desired career goals. The game meant following the men's rules by putting our careers above our children and doing everything possible not to bring our family problems to work with us. After all, the good old boys do not have time for such nonsense.

Of course, everybody knows that most mothers would never sacrifice their children in such a cruel manner; therefore, we might as well settle down and get on the "mommy track." How clever. Sounds like the train on that track is headed to the looney bin.

Never sacrifice the children for the buck.

This type of attitude is not only an insult to women but to the millions of men who take parenting as seriously as we do. Mommy tracking is a form of pigeonholing. It's prejudging and squelching the human spirit. It's a way to suppress the potentially great talent and versatility that both men and women who juggle family and career possess.

Give credit where credit is due. The twenty-first century family is a highly creative team whose priorities are straight. True, we are not perfect. We know we have plenty to learn, but we are breaking ground fast. We refuse to be intimidated and pigeonholed by mommy tracks and ornery good old boys because we know such tactics suppress all human potential.

There are surveys now that already indicate women who followed the good old boys' example—giving up family and focusing entirely on career—are suffering the same consequences that their role models have: early heart attacks, depression, alcoholism, and drug abuse. The good old boys sound bad to me.

We know that following those old rules would not have worked for us, so we made up our own in an attempt to discover a better way. It's not the perfect solution, but every new generation comes closer to achieving more balanced lives than those who came before.

Mothers Against Being Flat Broke

I am not ashamed to admit that I've always hated being broke. I detested standing in a checkout line with a baby on each hip and a knot in my stomach waiting for the clerk to hit the total button on the cash register. I knew I would not have enough money to pay for everything on the conveyor belt and would have to put things back on the shelf. People behind me in line would give me dirty looks. This was always extremely humiliating to me.

I hated having my phone, water, and lights turned off and lying to my kids by telling them "there must be some mistake." You see, my hatred about being broke, about having no money, has truly motivated me to focus on making the buck.

This was the case with many of us in this book. There was no one else to bail us out. There was no Prince Charming who was going to show up. There was no parents' trust fund we could tap. There was only one person on earth we could count on to change our fate—ourselves.

To say we were highly motivated is almost an understatement. Such intense motivation is the key to making necessary changes. The following stories of mothers who love money are shared to encourage you to get out of debt, possibly get an education or training, and support yourself and your family in the manner you all so richly deserve. Don't worry about getting too greedy. The final chapter in this book will help you put a check on yourself if you tend to be getting out of control.

Training and experience lead to earning power.

When it comes to having a strong desire to make money, there is no one I interviewed who felt motivated earlier in life to make a buck than dancer/choreographer Pauline Kyne. She was just a little girl growing up on the wrong side of the tracks in northern England when she first felt her family's heavy financial burdens.

"My desire to be the best dancer in all of England came from the realization that I was from a poor family. My family's only chance of breaking out of the lower middle class in England and getting over here rested on my shoulders."

The only way anyone could raise oneself and family economically was through education, but for the lower middle class in England in the 1940s and 1950s, it was not easy to be afforded that opportunity, no matter how smart you were.

"At ten or eleven, every student in public school sat for the scholarship. And if you failed the scholarship at ten years old, you never went to high school. You were stuck. It was the lot of the lower class."

There would be two days of cross-examination. Students were tested on their academic skills such as math, geography, and history.

Pauline failed the test by a few points. She knew in her heart how wrong it was to be judged and pigeonholed that way. All of these painful experiences endowed her with a superhuman desire to lift her family's financial burden. And that's exactly what she did.

By the time Pauline was twelve, she had become quite an accomplished dancer and was competing all over England and taking home first-place ribbons.

"I saw this as our ticket out of England. Academically, I had lost the chance to get to high school, so I had to raise our standards through my dancing talent."

But more obstacles fell on her path, driving her ambition deeper.

"When I was twelve, I went to London for the All-England Dance Competition. I remember somebody saying to me from my area, 'When you go down to London keep your mouth shut!' Evidently the people from London thought they were the cream of the crop and people like me from Yorkshire were not worth a damn because we were from the north."

But Pauline was not used to keeping her mouth shut.

"I arrived in London with my dancing teacher and another friend. I was the only one competing from my school. When my dancing teacher went into the competition hall to hand in my music, I walked into the dressing room and saw a few girls in costume at the table. I asked them if I could put my bag down next to their bags at an empty spot on the table."

They took one look at Pauline and promptly picked up their cases and walked to the other side of the room.

"I was left standing alone on one side of the room. There were literally seventy-five other kids on the other side of that room with their mothers just glaring at me. It was so humiliating."

She asked her dance teacher what she did wrong. Why did everyone move away from her? Her teacher told her the girls picked up her northern accent and they looked down upon people from the north. It became clear to Pauline that it all boiled down to one's status. Her spirit of competition rose to peak levels.

"My attitude was, 'I will show them. I am going to nail this dance, and my marks will be so far above the rest that it will embarrass them.' Even in the lineup as we stood there, no one would stand next to me."

She felt she was representing her family and the whole north of England. "I was on fire. I *had* to win." And she did. But even on stage after the performance when she accepted the trophy, the other dancers would not stand anywhere near her. More fuel was added to Pauline's fire when she was later accepted into the Royal Ballet Academy, receiving a first-year scholarship.

"But my family couldn't afford to pay for the other two years. I could find no sponsors to back me, and I lost the scholarship."

That defeated her temporarily.

"I thought there was no way out. I was really angry. I was blocked because of money. The next day, I made up my mind to leave England. I didn't know where I was going to go. Not only was I going to get myself out but also my parents and brothers."

Her dancing teacher's brother had immigrated to Canada and married a singer who was on a television show called *The Hit Parade*, so she knew she could get a job dancing on the show.

When Pauline was sixteen, she went alone by boat to Canada. She borrowed $150 from her uncle whom she promised to pay back. She landed a $255-a-week job dancing on Canada's popular *The Hit Parade*, and paid back her uncle immediately.

She became one of Canada's most popular television singer/dancers. Her talents gave her the earning power to bail her entire family out of England. "I brought my dad over first. He was free at last from the iron and steelworks in England. It was very brave of him and my mom to accept the ticket I sent. He left mom and my brothers and sisters behind but only temporarily. I told my mother not to worry, that I would send her the same amount of money Dad earned weekly. Then, once Dad got a job, we would find a place and bring the rest of them over within the year."

Her father got a job in television, painting sets, working on props, and doing other odd jobs. They both saved every penny they could.

"We used to delight in putting our checks together to see what we could afford to buy that week. At the same time that we were saving for the family's tickets, we were buying kitchen utensils, bedding, etc."

Pauline and her dad never used a charge card. They paid cash for everything they bought, never buying more than was needed. By the time she was nineteen, she had financed her entire family's crossing from England.

"Then we all put our money together and bought a three-bedroom house with a basement, which my mom eventually turned into a dance studio to accommodate all of her students. My brothers went on to get their education and became very successful businessmen. None of this would have been possible if we had stayed back in England."

In spite of Pauline later marrying a successful television director who earned an excellent income, it was always a given in her mind that she would work to make money and raise their three children side by side with him.

Ruth Harkin has a similar mind-set. The granddaughter of German immigrants, Ruth grew up with a strong work ethic.

"All my dad's sisters were nurses. Their families and their careers were both important. When we all got together at traditional Thanksgiving and Christmas dinners, their husbands would be typically in charge of dinners because the women were making extra money for Christmas gifts by working holiday shifts at the hospital."

Ruth's take on money may be different than many women. "Growing up, I fully expected to support myself. When I was contemplating getting married, I never expected anyone besides myself to support me. I like to work, and I like the reward that doing a good job pays."

Ruth's husband, Senator Tom Harkin (D-Iowa), is more motivated by "legislative achievements and making a difference in people's lives on a national and global level." Is this a bone of contention in the Harkin marriage?

"Not at all," says Ruth. "It actually works out in my favor. He is much more domesticated than I am. I haven't cooked or cleaned since our children were born. My family does not see me in the same terms as other mothers. They see me as the mover and shaker and the one who makes things happen. I delegate well, too."

Understanding the importance of money hasn't hurt one of America's most influential women, Judith Regan. Her early motivation moved her through a $1.60-an-hour job scooping Carvel ice cream to being one of the "100 most powerful" people in the entertainment business as the president and publisher of the Regan Company and Regan Books, and the host of her own show on the Fox News Channel. Her list of published work includes: Wally Lamb's *She's Come Undone*, Fran Drescher's *Enter Whining*, and Dr. Barry Sears's *The Zone*.

"My motivation to succeed and make money came about in part because I need to feel secure. I wasn't born with a trust fund and I don't ever want to stay in a bad relationship with a man or an employer again—that is one of the benefits of being financially secure."

When her former publisher Simon and Schuster didn't offer the entrepreneurial atmosphere she craved, Regan negotiated a sweet deal with mogul Rupert Murdoch and the

News Corporation, allowing her to produce projects in all mediums—from film to television to publishing.

"I am ambitious and have always wanted to be financially independent. There were five kids in our family, and my father was an elementary schoolteacher. The most money he made a year was around thirty thousand dollars. So there was never enough money to do anything. In my family, if you wanted to do something, you had to figure out how to make the money to pay for it."

Regan says her motivation to do a good job and be paid well has produced within her a boundless energy.

In today's world, she believes it's easy for women to become financially successful. "Start wherever you can. If you have to go to McDonald's and flip hamburgers, do the best job you can. Before long you will be managing the place. Most people today do not know how to do a good job. It's easy to get noticed when you do a good job."

"If you put in the hours providing excellent service and working with a good attitude, you will *succeed*! It is that simple."

Judith, Ruth, Pauline, and I all *had* to work. We possessed built-in motivation. Some stay-at-home wives argue that they aren't motivated to make money because there is no need to. After all, their husbands bring home plenty.

"It's dangerous business to act as if you are entitled to be taken care of by a man financially," says Judith Regan. "I always wanted to take care of myself, no matter what. Women need to think twice about sitting back and letting the man take care of them. It's pure fantasy to think some guy is going to come along and take care of you and pay all the bills while you stay home and raise the kids.

"They may say they want to do that in the beginning of the relationship to lure you in, but eventually they resent it. If the relationship ends in divorce, it is rare that a man willingly supports his ex-wife and children. So women need to find a way to make their own money, and they need to make money a priority. As my friend Georgette Mosbacher says of men and money: A woman's attitude should be, 'I don't need your money, honey.'"

Divorce isn't always the issue. Even if the marriage was made in heaven, spouses rarely die simultaneously. One living partner may be left to handle all the affairs. For the woman who has never worked or paid much attention to the management of money, this could be a devastating financial blow to the family.

Take Rosemary Garbett, she was a high school graduate who married at eighteen and left every decision up to her husband, claiming she was a "very dominated housewife."

In 1976, her husband Thomas accidentally shot himself to death, leaving Rosemary in charge of four children, $250,000 in debts, and $20,000 in life insurance. Rosemary's accountant and lawyer advised her to sell her husband's chain of Houston restaurants appraised at $800,000.

She was offered half of the appraised price but decided not to sell. She had four kids to raise, and she figured she would have to work three or four jobs to keep going.

With no credit history of her own, at first she couldn't get any bank to give her a much-needed loan to improve the business. What happened? Out of desperation, Rosemary became a good manager and a successful businesswoman. Today, at sixty, she oversees five profitable Mexican restaurants, and sales have grown from $1.5 million to almost $5 million.

She says what saved her was knowing how to balance the books.

It Doesn't Grow on Trees

I used to think being money motivated and then going out and bringing home the bacon was my only responsibility in terms of the stewardship of money. I inherited my parents' strong work ethic. Both my parents grew up during the aftermath of the Depression. But from the same experience, they both brought very different viewpoints on money into their adult lives.

My father's view, which he passed on to me, was, "Spend it as fast as you can make it, babe. Who knows? The banks might go under and then it won't be worth the damn paper it's printed on." He loved dressing to the nines, wearing expensive suits, driving brand-new Cadillacs, and eating at the finest restaurants.

His spending habits truly aggravated my mom, who lived through the horrors of the Depression with my Italian-immigrant grandparents. I grew up in my grandparents' downstairs flat of their two-story house in Chicago. The story of how they almost lost their home, which they scrimped and saved for back in 1922, was often repeated at our house, especially after one of my dad's spending sprees.

"Your grandfather didn't make much money being a tailor. And your grandmother worked in a factory, but they saved $7,000 to buy this house. Something that is never going to happen if your dad keeps pissing money away like this.

"In 1933, at the height of the Depression, they almost lost this place. They missed making one of their monthly $100 house payments, and the owner was going to foreclose.

"Your grandparents could barely write or read English. I read in the newspaper that if a family could prove they were a hardship case, the government would pay off the loans in bonds and make the present owners a twenty-year mortgage.

"So when I was a sophomore in high school, I wrote President Roosevelt a letter to see if my parents would qualify."

Within three weeks, Mom got a letter that the government would take over their mortgage under the new Federal Home Owners Loan Corporation.

"Other than owning that house, my parents didn't have a pot to pee in. So when I see your father spending it like he's got it, it makes me truly nervous."

Dad died in 1978. Mother is alive and well at 82, living in a home she owns free and clear out in Sun City, Nevada. She still clips coupons and turns them in at the local grocery store.

Over the years she slowly but surely saved enough money in the bank to live very comfortably for the rest of her life and cover any emergency health problems.

"I am not going to be one of those old ladies that has to burden her daughter with my financial problems. Your father never earned more than $18,000 a year. But he was a smart man because he knew money went through his hands like water. So at one point he turned over his checkbook to me and told me never to allow him to write another check again. I gave him a weekly allowance. From his paycheck I always saved money.

Save.

My only regret is that I didn't give her my checkbook about twenty years ago. If I did, I probably would have a "Pot to Pee in" by now, myself. You see, I've inherited what Mom called Dad's "high off the hog" attitude about money. I may be a slow learner, but I am not stupid. Finally I am following my mother's advice: "You know, Danielle. Money doesn't grow on trees."

And I am finally learning how to live below my means.

LIVING BELOW YOUR MEANS

Jim Rhode (Naomi's husband) says working parents get into trouble by living above their means.

"Since 1980, our income has been quite generous with Naomi's added paychecks. But we haven't touched them for the past ten years. All her pay goes into a fund that she does not see or spend. We pride ourselves on living below our means, but we live well."

Jim says working mothers and dads need to identify what their money problems are and then work to reduce that debt and pressure.

"People get off the beaten track and live way too high. Everybody needs to learn that Rome was not built in a day. The inability to practice delayed gratification causes undue family financial pressure. The more you learn to delay gratification, the richer you will be in all aspects of your life."

Senator Tom Harkin and his wife Ruth support the Rhodes' philosophy on money. "Money is not an issue at our house. Because of our backgrounds we were never used to a lot of money. We do not harbor expensive tastes. I am fifty-seven years old, and I have never had a new car. I always buy used cars or when Ruth gets finished with her car, I take it."

Steward money.

The Harkins have never kept track of who was making more money. "It's gone back and forth. The important thing is we have always had enough to meet our needs, and beyond that, we saved to send our kids to good colleges."

Like the Rhodes, Tom and Ruth Harkin know the value of practicing delayed gratification.

"We have forgone certain accruements of life for the bigger picture. We were married in 1967, ate off a card table and chairs until 1975. Many young couples start off their marriage accumulating things. They have to have furniture, new cars. Then, they borrow and that puts them under so much pressure."

Nancy Hays says, "Historically, I have been cheap, and I live cheap. I drive an old car and I save money. Maybe it comes from those days right after college when I was poor and traveling on the road as a singer. I also had very frugal parents."

Candice and Doug Brooks ran on a fast money track in the beginning of their marriage.

"We pushed the envelope financially. We tried to keep up with the Joneses. We left no margin for error, and we were going to lose it all. Plus, we had no money in the bank for our retirement."

When they were expecting their first child, they began downscaling.

Downscale.

"Thank goodness we got our wake-up call early. My advice to working moms and dads is to get rid of some of that financial burden. Our goal is now no longer to be upwardly mobile.

"I used to validate myself for being upwardly mobile. What's so cool about killing yourself? We want time more than money. One day, Doug and I looked at each other and said, 'If we were really so smart and so good at what we did, we would have tons of time off.'"

They no longer wanted to strangle themselves financially.

"If we can't go skiing or go for a mountain-bike ride in between all the work, then what is the point? That is why we moved to this mountain community.

"I don't want to wait until I am sixty-five. We ask ourselves, 'What do we need financially to get by and be happy?' and 'What can we do without?'"

Downscaling and using money to buy more time sounds like a simple process, but Candice says there were a lot of temptations luring them back to their old habits.

"Doug and I were with a huge international company for six years, which involved lots of international travel, trips that would keep us on the road for two or three weeks at a time. We were spokespeople who were paid huge amounts of money, so it was hard to let go of that contract.

"When you get used to bringing in a certain amount of money, it is hard to say no. But both of us knew deep down we were compromising priorities."

When renewal time came up, the Brookses said no. "But it was tough because the money was secure. If we had said yes, I would be going to South America and going to Europe, which is not what I wanted to do, especially at our kids' ages."

"Because we said no at the appropriate time in our growth as a family, other opportunities fell into place for Doug and me that were more in line with our family goals. These opportunities just wouldn't have happened if we had renewed that old contract. Now I can stay home and write scripts and produce videos. I can't do that on the road."

These days, they are much more accountable for the money they earn.

"When we go on vacation, we no longer opt for the $350-a-night hotel room. A bed and breakfast is just fine. It's no longer hard to make these kinds of decisions because we feel the absence of financial pressure in our lives."

Sharon D'Orsie says it's not the money spent but the time spent together that counts. "Forget about having an expensive vacation. The money only goes so far. I took my kids camping, in state parks for years. They loved it. The real turning point was when I took them to Washington, D.C., one Christmas.

"I used the opportunity to sightsee, and when my son Charlie was asked what he liked best about the vacation, he said he liked sleeping somewhere besides his room and eating potato chips. I said to myself, *We can do the same thing much cheaper by camping out in state parks, and I'll bring the potato chips.*

"What I see in my neighborhood are these young couples with flashy cars and expensive houses. Then they take the whole family to the Club Med. These same children are ending up with uncaring, illiterate caretakers who are paid next to nothing for assisting in the raising of the children while their parents work.

"There was a couple in our town who were both medical professionals and had a beautiful house in the 'burbs and two gorgeous toddlers. But their housekeeper was young and irresponsible, and both children ended up drowning in the swimming pool of their expensive house. Nobody was watching over them closely."

Check your own spending and you will save big money.

Making the right money choices is a critical part of our juggling routine. Every aspect of how we make and spend our money has to be examined.

TERRY SAVAGE'S FINANCIAL STRATEGIES FOR FAMILIES

To help you (and me) learn how to keep our hands on some of this money we earn, I asked financial wizard Terry Savage to give us some sound financial advice.

"Few two-income couples take full advantage of their financial power. And they don't concentrate on making their money work for them. Think about it. If you both were living separately, you would each have rent or mortgage payments, phone, utility bills. And it wouldn't be as much fun to dine at home.

"So don't spend all your double income. Use it to your advantage. There are two types of people: savers and spenders. For better or worse, they tend to marry each other. The result is often conflicting views of money and how it should be spent and invested.

"To make matters more stressful, both adults in dual-income households usually are aggressive about having their own way."

Terry says the result is two people trying to control each other's financial behavior in ways that generate conflict. There is a better way.

"Instead, sit down with your partner and confront your money attitudes. Then discuss how best to handle your finances. Take a close look at your overall financial picture. Ask yourselves:

- How much of your respective incomes do you want to save?
- What are your savings goals (vacation, new car, down payment on a house, college for the kids, retirement)?
- Should you be accountable to each other for all of your spending, or should you each have a private account?
- How many credit cards will you use? Or will you cut up all but one of your cards and take a weekly cash allowance?

Terry says another way to limit the amount of damage done by reckless spending habits is "to set up separate accounts for a portion of your earnings. Pay your household expenses out of one joint account."

She cautions us to remember that, depending on the state where we live, we may be responsible for our spouse's debts, and our spouse's bill-paying habits could affect our credit reports.

In many households, the financial chores are divided. One person pays the bills and balances the checkbook while the other invests and organizes the taxes. But Terry says, "It is far better if both of you understand and are responsible for all aspects of your finances."

"An added benefit is if the spender had to balance the checkbook and pay the bills, he/she might not be so willing to buy impulsively. If the person who handles the checkbook understood more about investing, he would probably better understand why it is so important to make out that monthly check to the mutual fund to save for college or retirement."

Terry has counseled hundreds of couples and knows that often they each have different views about how to handle their income taxes and organize their records, especially if they prepare their own tax returns.

"You may be an aggressive filer who claims every deduction, while your spouse may be more conservative for fear of triggering an audit. If both of you sign the return, both of you are liable for any mistakes, disallowances (when the IRS doesn't allow a deduction), or penalties.

"Seek professional tax filing help. Find a CPA who makes both of you comfortable. It may be worth the extra expense to give you peace of mind about your taxes."

It's good to remember that two-income households may not always have those two incomes. "If that is the case, right now you have power, leverage, and maneuverability. A spouse could take time off to change careers or go back to school. Or what if one of you loses your job?

"Think of spending less now not as a penalty but as a form of deferred consumption. It's a real bonus. Remember, if you don't see the money, you won't spend it. Start automatic monthly deductions from your paycheck or checking account into a stock market mutual fund. Let your money work as hard for you, as you work for it."

Set up automatic deductions from your checking account.

You and I aren't the only ones who have to get smarter about money. Too often I have found myself reaching into my pocket and giving my children money for frivolous items that I know they would not purchase if the money used was their own hard-earned cash. This example came up a few months back when a friend and I took our daughters shopping in Salt Lake City at one of our favorite shopping haunts, "Nordies" (for the uneducated shopper, the translation is Nordstrom's Department Store).

Kathleen had taken some of her own money out of her savings account to spend. By the end of the shopping spree, my designated cash was all gone, but Kath was still in the money. She had a "whim" (to quote her father) to buy another pair of earrings and a matching hair clip. Of course, she wanted me to buy it for her.

I told her the bank was closed. She started whining a bit, and of course I found the perfect retort: "Why not use your own money?"

Next thing I noticed, she is over in the corner counting her greenbacks and then putting them back in her change purse. We all started walking out of the store when I stopped and said, "Oh, Kath, what about the earrings and hair clip? Aren't you going to buy those?"

"Naw," says she. "I thought of something I want more than that junk."

Just think. I could have ended up spending my own hard-earned pesos on that "junk." It's funny how some people's desires wane when they have to dip into their own pockets.

Nancy Hays says she has to watch herself when it comes to buying unnecessary trinkets and toys for her kids. "If I don't spend the time with them, it doesn't work to try and buy back those hours with toys and clothes. All kids really want is our time and attention. A lot of this guilt about not bringing home tons of boxes of gifts for them, especially after a business trip, is guilt that is in my head."

Give your children a money lesson.

Children of working mothers and dads need to know why we work and how the money we make works.

Terry Savage says, "When my son was twelve, I set him straight about what the green stuff was all about. I did not spend extra money on him because I felt guilty about working. This is a huge mistake working mothers make and then they get those charge cards building and find themselves in bigger pickles.

"I told my son the government takes 40 percent of every penny I make. In layman's language, if I make $50,000 a year, the first $20,000 is going to Uncle Sam."

He couldn't believe Uncle Sam got so much of his mother's money. Terry told him someday he was going to face the same issues, and it is the price we pay to live in the land of the free.

"I made it clear he knew that someday he was going to take over the responsibility of making money and taking care of himself, so he better get a good education.

"Then I told him what the financial arrangement would be on his education. He gets four years of his college tuition paid by me. But not one quarter or one semester more. If he did not finish in four years, then he could figure out how to pay for the rest.

"The day he turns twenty-one, he is on his own. Then I started laying out for him what the cost of raising him meant in today's economy:

	per year
Housekeeper . . . . =	$25,000
Food (*his portion*) . . . . =	$6,000
Rent (*his portion*) . . . . =	$15,000
Tuition . . . . =	$30,000

"Forgetting the cost of rent per month, the tuition alone is going to equal a minimum of $30,000 for the year. Then I told him to add all these expenses up. Next, I asked him to remember that I pay 40 percent of my income to taxes due to my tax bracket.

Give the children a list of monthly expenses.

"So we figured the first $80,000 a year that I make goes to taking care of him. And that does not count living expenses, such as clothes. So I told him to figure when he graduates from college, he needs to make at least $40,000 to $50,000.

"Then I explained to him that is the reason why I am not always home on time for dinner. I did not want to put him down or make him feel guilty; I just wanted him to understand the cost of things.

"I gave him an allowance, and I did not make a big deal out of it. And I did open accounts for him. We had stocks that he would follow. When he was nine years old, he bought Ralston Purina stock at $11 a share. We bought that because that is what we fed the dog. He read the stock market in the paper and he watched his stock double. So I said, 'Let's sell!'

Invest.

"I think it went to 30 or 32. He said to me, 'No, Mom, I don't want to sell!' He was paying attention. Today, he is a financial man, and he calls me and tells me to do the same thing I told him to do when he was nine years old: 'Mom, we have to buy 100 shares.'"

Terry says there is a fine line between creating guilt in your children and just educating them on the fact that money does not grow on trees.

"I never discussed this with the intention of creating guilt. I merely wanted my son to have a realistic picture of what things cost. We lived very well because of my vocation. House in the country. He got to bring his friends. He went to great summer camps. I wanted him to understand the relationship between work and money and taxes and things.

"I am in the financial education business. He needed to know how much I make, spend, and the tax bracket I am in."

The lesson is if you are going to be successful, the government is going to pick your pocket for 40 percent or more. A median family now pays 33 percent of income to taxes for state and federal. So half of what you make is gone.

"It is important to teach our children the trade-off between work and money. Recognize that we are not making all that money. The government takes 40 percent of it.

"Plus we have a whole generation of kids who sit in backseats of their mothers' cars and see Mom pull up to a drive-through window and put a card through a machine and out comes twenty-dollar bills. In the old days, I used to do a TV show to educate kids about money that was called *It Doesn't Grow on Trees*.

"Now I would call it, *It Doesn't Come out of Cash Machines*."

After my interview with Terry, I couldn't help but think about all the money working mothers have paid out in income taxes. Recently, in writer Ellen Goodman's commentary on the double hit working couples get on income taxes, she applauded Ed McCaffery. He is an economist and law professor and the author of *Taxing Women*.

Goodman writes, "Today's conservatives say women have been forced to work to pay confiscatory taxes. But McCaffery shows how the tax laws favor traditional single-earner families. They have a built-in prejudice against married working mothers."

When two-income families file their tax returns, they tend to look at the wife's income as "a secondary earner." The secondary earners are taxed at a higher rate.

"Assume, for example, an upper-income man earns $100,000 a year. The first $16,000 he earns is tax free. But when her $30,000 income is put on top of his, every one of her dollars is taxed at his highest rate. When you subtract Social Security, state, and local taxes, she is taking home $15,000."

Of course, that does not include child-care and other working expenses. This whole tax situation escalates in upper-middle-income households.

McCaffery says to right the issue, "at least alter the Social Security payments and benefits, and provide a deduction for child-care costs. One of the worst features of our times is that women are divided and conflicted within themselves and among each other while men just march merrily along."

In conclusion, I wish to propose a solution to all the working mothers' problems worldwide. Tell those who hire you or your bosses to pay you double for your work. Then you'll have plenty of extra dough left over to pay taxes.

Double your income.

Here's my rationale: No matter what our occupation may be, there are individuals doing the exact same thing we do, taking the exact same amount of time, and they are receiving the exact same money.

But they do not work the second shift (family) like we do. So just double our money because we're worth it.

CHAPTER SIX

Together We Shall Overcome

One of my heroes is the late Bishop Fulton J. Sheen. Some of you mothers who grew up in the fifties like me may have watched his weekly television show, *Life Is Worth Living*. I have some of Sheen's final television sermons on videotape. Whenever I start making mountains out of molehills, I watch one in particular that sets me straight.

He began by writing a Greek word on the blackboard: *skolop*. He explained the word meant "a handicap, a thorn, or a stimulus of the flesh." Then he reminded his listeners that a *skolop* could be anything: an emotional handicap, a difficult marriage, hard-to-manage children. But it really doesn't matter. What matters is what we decide to do with the burden.

Then he proposed that if it were possible, he would have each member of the audience come up on stage and lay their burden down for all to see. Once everybody had the chance to see another's burden, they'd have a choice—trade someone else for their skolop or take back their own.

A spellbinding storyteller, Sheen knew how to use the pregnant pause to his advantage. After he threw out the option, he silently stood in the middle of the stage, scrutinizing what seemed like every face in the crowd.

Then, suddenly, with a dramatic burst of Sheen passion, he opened his robed arms wide and interrogated us with a deeply compelling, yet lovingly compassionate voice, "You'd gladly take back your own . . . Wouldn't you?"

Every time I listen to that part of his sermon, I feel like a stupid, spoiled brat. One question, posed with Sheen's strength of conviction, had the power to pull the masses out of complacency. We all need reminders of how lucky we are on some level when we start to lose our most valuable possession: an attitude of gratitude.

> There is always the opportunity to turn trials into blessings. It's your choice.

Knowing how important keeping that attitude is, especially in the midst of overcoming obstacles, I collected stories from certain courageous moms who had every reason in the world to throw in the towel but turned every one of their trials into blessings.

True Grit Mama

I learned about Betty Browner from one of her three sons. At the time, she was a seventy-one-year-old lawyer. When we finally talked, she reminded me of a female Rocky with a Lucille Ball deep voice, who won many of life's toughest battles.

Betty married an alcoholic some fifty-eight years ago, bore three sons with him, and got divorced when the boys were two, four, and six. At the time, her home was going into foreclosure. She had no job, no education, and was dead broke. Her first step to independence was enrolling in real estate school.

She bought a German shepherd dog, taught herself how to drive a car, packed the boys and the dog up in her MG, and went around the neighborhood listing houses like a tornado. It pulled her out of poverty.

Her next career began when she met the inventor of a miniature crystal earphone radio. He and Betty decided to go into business together. They opened up an electronics toy company that exclusively employed socially and physically handicapped people.

That business supported her family for the next several years while she and the boys went to college. She graduated after she turned forty-six, then decided to go to law school at forty-seven. She got this idea when she owned the electronics firm because she was always dealing with incompetent lawyers. She was positive she knew more about representing herself than they did.

This gets even better. While Betty was in undergraduate school, two of her three sons finished college, got married, started having their own children, and they all moved in with her. She said it was tough for them to make it financially. One of her boys was in law school, too, and he couldn't have become a lawyer if he and his family hadn't moved in with mom to help them get going.

She claimed the whole bunch of them got along great but admitted it got pretty wild at times. Everybody was trying to study, and there were babies crawling all over the place. Eventually, one by one, each one of her sons got his feet on the ground, moved out, and made his mark in the world. She said she is so proud and so thrilled to have had the privilege of helping them out.

The lessons on how to overcome obstacles from this true grit mother are many.

Quit feeling sorry for yourself and start using your talents. Betty represents mostly men in her law practice. "Women drive me nuts. They get divorced, have no job skills, and come to me wanting to clean their husband's clock. Some women end up with $300,000 settlements and still complain how that isn't enough because they gave these men the best years of their lives. Why didn't they use their talents the best years of their lives?"

> **Quit feeling sorry for yourself and take action.**

Always look at the upside of a situation. Isn't everything a trade-off? Betty said it is terrific that single moms do not have to consult with a man when a decision comes up. She always consulted with her sons. "We made good decisions together."

Another upside of being single is that single moms are never put in the middle between a man and a child because the dad wants attention. She thinks there is often less tension in a single parent's house. "They never heard their dad and me battling it out behind closed doors."

Betty says when a single mother is well adjusted to her life with her children and job, the household functions much saner than one that is occupied by a man and woman who do not belong together.

Look for great male role models. Betty tried to hire male babysitters as much as possible. It was expensive, but she sent her boys to a 49ers football camp when they were little.

Have a sense of humor and be a friend to your kids. Betty used to take her boys to football games and on vacations galore, and she built her social life around them.

Laugh until it hurts.

"A sense of humor is a mother's saving grace. We used to have a hoot. Sometimes we'd get to messing around and they would lock me out of the house in my nightgown and throw the backyard floodlight on me. I'd be screaming, 'You brats better let me back in!'"

Don't leak emotions out in front of the kids. One time when Betty was broke, she was in her kitchen, crying to a neighbor about how she' had nothing. Her three-year-old overheard and came into the room, sat on her lap, and said, "You have me, Mommy."

After that comment she vowed never to pull that type of thing in front of her children again.

Take action. Betty believes single mothers sometimes lack self-confidence to pick up the phone and act on their ideas or intuition.

"When my neighbor told me about real estate school, I did something about it immediately. Don't wait until all conditions are perfect. Women do this often and end up immobilized, just sitting around the kitchen table staring into space. Get gutsy. Enroll in class. Write the letter. Arrange an interview. Force yourself out of oblivion."

Be brave.

NEVER SAY NEVER

Kelly Radaker Jones and her husband purposely wanted to miss what our Jazz Dad in Chapter 2 considered the experience of his lifetime: parenthood. Their careers and being married to each other provided plenty of fulfillment for them. But those biological clocks tend to kick in, don't they? Suddenly, the women with the most glamorous careers who kept saying, "No way, no how" to motherhood in their twenties question that decision by the time they're in their early thirties.

Here's what happened to Kelly.

"I was one of four children in a close and loving family. My father was the epitome of the American Dream. A true self-made man. He and my mother met when they were twelve and thirteen. He made and lost and made again several fortunes. She was a stay-at-home mom. But I always sensed, growing up, as wonderful a mom as she was that she felt there was something lacking in her life in terms of her creative needs and what she could have done to develop herself.

"She is an extremely intelligent woman and in this day and age, she probably would have had a successful career, too."

Kelly did not want to choose the path of staying home and having kids.

"My husband and I met in graduate school, and he felt exactly the same way. We were madly in love with each other and our work. We were very sure of ourselves when it came to knowing we did *not* want a family."

They got their Ph.D.'s together in industrial psychology, then moved to Boston and started their careers. Kelly worked at a consulting firm. Her husband Robert went to work for a bank.

"After we were married for a few years and right before we finished our doctorate work, I began thinking about having a child. All the focus was suddenly off this education thing, and I started to think differently about my life."

She went to the doctor for a checkup and found out her chances of becoming pregnant were very slim.

"I thought, *That's it. By God, I am going to do it.*"

For the next eight years, the couple that didn't want to have a child tried desperately to conceive one. But did Kelly's husband also shift gears? "It was unbelievable. He seemed to change his mind around the same time as I did. He was great about going and taking the necessary tests."

For the next several years, their careers thrived in the midst of Kelly's surgeries, fertility shots, and prescriptions. The month she turned thirty, they moved to California so Robert could start his own distribution company. And that was the month she found out she was finally pregnant.

A few weeks later, complications set in and in the middle of a business meeting she started to miscarry. Ultimately, she lost the baby.

After that heartbreak, they went through four more years of trying to have a baby.

"Back and forth to the fertility clinic. Finally we tried in vitro. Nothing was working, and Robert felt he couldn't go through this anymore."

They sat down and decided they were missing the point.

"We were so lucky to have each other. We had a wonderful family and great nieces and nephews. I said that if this wasn't right for us, we could be the best aunt and uncle going. So we decided to count our blessings and concentrate on what we had."

They were at peace with that decision. When the in vitro fertilization didn't work, they forgot about having a child. Robert and Kelly went into practice together and developed customized training for executives in some of America's top companies. Her specialty was change management, and she was more and more in demand.

One fall they were in Salem, Massachusetts, with a client and staying at the beautiful Nathaniel Hawthorne Hotel.

"We were having a grand time personally and professionally. Very romantic and a profitable business trip. Six weeks later, I had to go back to the same hotel for a business meeting. This time, Robert was at home in L.A. We were talking on the phone, and I don't know what possessed him to bring this up, but he asked if something was wrong with my menstrual cycle. He reminded me I hadn't had a period for quite a while."

She hung up the phone and thought maybe she should make an appointment. She had thrown out her thermometer and had stopped keeping track of her periods on the calendar.

"But I got this funny feeling. I had a dinner engagement but decided to run down to the corner drugstore and pick up one of those pregnancy tests. In a split second, the stick turned blue.

"I will never forget that moment. I called Robert back in L.A., not knowing what his reaction would be. He was totally thrilled. We both started crying over the phone. We knew we had conceived our child at this exact hotel a few short months ago."

Count your blessings.

Her pregnancy was easy, and she traveled and worked up until she delivered her son Jordan. Then, eight and a half months later, she conceived Rachel. Two babies, one and a half years apart. Not bad for a focused career woman who started out never wanting children, then changing her mind, only to find out she had a fertility problem. Never say never, ladies.

Kelly shares lessons learned while overcoming obstacles in her life:

Choose to be grateful for what you have. The moral of Bishop Sheen's story is true for Kelly and Robert, too. "It was always my choice to say I am so lucky because I have a wonderful marriage and husband, and I'm able to work on projects I love to do. I have seen infertility destroy marriages. Every month, going through that disappointment of getting another period. You must make the choice to focus on what you have.

> **Cherish the moment. Give thanks for every detail of your present situation.**

"When I turned grateful, I found peace and the family I wanted so badly. This is something we teach to our children, too. Whenever they start complaining, I tell them to concentrate on the toys that they do have. Starting with those little things builds character later."

While riding the rough waters, keep talking to each other. Remember Kathy Smith telling us how she and her husband took walks and confronted the sticky subjects? So did Kelly and Robert.

"It takes courage not to sweep stuff under the carpet. I did not suspect Robert was having a hard time adjusting after those two babies came along—two babies inside of a year and a half for two people who were *never* going to have children.

"One day we were in the office, and he just blurted it out. He said, 'I do not know where I am anymore in this marriage. I love these children and you, but I do not feel real happy right now.'

"It got down to the pressure and the exhaustion we both felt after having our two children so close together. Originally, we had gotten along so well in all areas—our work being a big part of it.

"In a way, he was jealous of the kid thing because he has had this partner in work and life and suddenly he is sharing. That was the hardest adjustment. But he opened up and talked about it.

"It was especially rough after Rachel was born, but as time went on and I got back to my work, he saw that the woman he married had not abandoned him. We always have something to talk about that does not include the kids."

Learn how to wait. "Knowing how to wait has become an important asset in my life both at home and at work. Infertility taught me how to deal with my impatience. Once I conceived, I was forced to learn how to wait both during pregnancy and while my children grow. We have to let them figure some things out on their own, and this takes patience, too. Don't fight it. Relax and enjoy not knowing. You will end up with two benefits: the delayed gratification of receiving something or someone wonderful and the virtue of patience."

Wait and be patient.

Use the worst-case scenario technique to get back into the present moment. "One thing my father taught me that is a great tool. When I thought I would have to face the fact that I would never have children, he reminded me to ask myself the question, 'What is the worst thing that could happen?' That was when I knew that I would always have my wonderful husband Robert, an exciting career, and lots of close family."

By asking yourself that question, you are forced to look at what you are agonizing over right in the face. Sometimes I think the avoidance of looking at that so-called worst-case scenario is where the panic comes from.

Kelly feels she is more effective as a negotiator on the job now, too. The good negotiator can wait and do without, if necessary. With prospects who do not call her back immediately she often asks herself, *What happens if they do not call me back?*

"I answer myself with the worst-case scenario: I get another client. Or no one will ever call me again. So great. Robert is working, so if we have to live on one income, so be it. Lots of people do it."

She says life never plays out your worst-case scenario.

"And then, whatever happens works out, and it's always better than what you imagined."

GRADUATION WAS THEIR LIBERATION

But what happens if your life, temporarily at least, does play out your worst nightmare? Is there hope for a better future after the fact? Marissa Cobb Weaver knows there is plenty of reason to hope. Her parents migrated from the South to the Midwest when factories opened up in the North and people of color were trying to move up to a better life for themselves.

By the time Marissa was nine years old, her parents were divorced. Her mother came from a family of alcoholics. Marissa's mom had a severe drinking problem.

"My father left, and my mother could not go earn a living due to her drinking problem. I remember they turned off our electricity and heat from time to time in the middle of winter. We had to either boil water on a hot plate for bathing purposes or go to a friend's house to take a shower."

Her mother was on welfare, and by the time Marissa was sixteen she had a baby and was on welfare, too. She said she knows the reason she moved out and had a child that young was because things were so bad at home. Her mom's alcoholism became increasingly worse.

"Her male friends were at the house all the time. And the older I got, the more uncomfortable I became with the advances those men were making toward me. I just finally moved out."

Marissa found comfort in the arms of her twenty-year-old boyfriend.

"He was very cute and controlling. I found that very appealing because my home life was so out of control. He said he wanted to have a baby, and I said okay.

"My daughter was the miracle baby. She was born prematurely, at twenty-six weeks—one pound and six ounces. Due to my nutritionally deficient pregnancy, I got toxemia."

The future for her and her new family looked bleak. She dropped out of school in her junior year. But after the baby was born, she passed her high school equivalency test and got a full scholarship to Marquette University in Milwaukee.

"Before I dropped out of high school, I was a 4.0 student. Deep down, I wanted an education. I never wanted to stay on welfare or be like my mother."

Her newborn stayed in the hospital from February to July. Marissa was at Marquette being financed by a combination of scholarships and grants. At one point, the baby was given a high dose of medication through IVs and as a result had a cardiac arrest.

"She was three months old when she had the heart attack. Once we brought her home, she could not be left with babysitters. We had to hire a nurse. Then there was the weekly doctor's visit. And she had to remain on heart monitors for one year. Between trying to appease my boyfriend and take care of my daughter, I finally dropped out of school. At that point, I didn't have the discipline or the fight required to stay in college."

Her boyfriend was working on and off, doctor bills mounted, and they were on Title 19 assistance.

"People think if you are on welfare that it is a grant. But once you start working, you have to pay it back. We will be making monthly payments to the state of Wisconsin forever, but I am grateful the money was there for us."

Marissa was irrepressible. "Once we got married, it all went downhill from there. We were both minimum wage earners and still on welfare. He started emotionally and then physically abusing me. Luckily, I had worked in a bank and passed the insurance exam along the way. I worked as a bank teller by day and sold insurance at night."

The relationship kept roller-coastering for the next few years. They would separate and get back together.

"He would come by once a month and visit our daughter. On one of his visits, I got pregnant again. We decided to reconcile. I left my job because by then he was in the military and we were sent to Michigan. When I got up there, I found out he had a slew of girlfriends."

They stayed married for a while and Marissa sold mutual funds.

"I was making good money and my kids were healthy, so I overlooked a lot. But I kept wanting to go back to school. Then my girlfriend told me about Alverno weekend college in Milwaukee."

She enrolled and started driving back and forth every other weekend. That's when the physical abuse started. He never touched the children, only Marissa. And his affairs with women multiplied.

Marissa finally got the courage to walk out. "I left the day after our anniversary with $20 in my pocket. I didn't even tell him I was leaving. I moved in with my girlfriend. He kept the kids until I got a house and a job."

When one door closes, another opens.

I asked her if she felt guilty leaving her family with him.

"He was always good enough with the children that I felt comfortable, but I knew I needed to save myself. I could do nothing for those kids until I cleaned up my life."

Her real regret is that she once again agreed to reconcile with him. "I fell for his line. He said he missed me and he had changed. Plus I found out my babysitter had hit my daughter. I felt like I had no help, and I was so close to graduation. We both reconciled for the wrong reasons. I found out he came back because be was having big financial problems and needed money.

"The worst thing I did was let my children witness their father abusing me. I had convinced myself it was better to be there than to be gone, and so I was taking the abuse. Plus I was dead set against my children growing up in a single-parent household like I did. I heard the stats about girls from single-parent households being much more likely to get pregnant early. I did not want history to repeat itself."

Her entire senior year of college, her husband kept saying he knew she was going to leave him as soon as she got her degree.

"I would go off to college on the weekends. By then he would get a babysitter and go drinking and carousing with lots of women. Nobody saw him until Monday morning."

Her husband was still there the day she graduated. "I remember we had a party. I was absolutely elated. My family came up from Mississippi. Here I was, a former school dropout at the age of sixteen, pregnant, and on welfare. My family just never thought I would graduate from high school, much less college.

"My husband acted like he was possessed. He would not let me out of his sight. He came with me to the rehearsal. Didn't want me to go by myself. He selected the dress I was to wear. He embarrassed me so badly in front of my father because he wouldn't allow me to hand in my robe unless he came with me. This was an all-women's college. Only the women were allowed in the gym to take off our robes."

At the graduation party, he clung to her. When she said *hi* to a man who she worked with, her husband had a fit. "He gave me the full third degree. 'How do you know him? Why has he come? Why did you invite him?'"

His possessiveness was something she relished at sixteen. "I was too young and naive to realize this would become a major problem."

When did she finally stop the insanity in her life?

"Well, something finally snapped. It happened when I knew for sure he was seeing someone. I found the notes she wrote to him in his car visor. There were also receipts for roses he had sent to her. This was all going on when I was working three jobs and in my last year of college. Plus I think graduation was my liberation."

Thirty days after she graduated, he was gone. He's never been back since. After she graduated from college, she went away for eleven weeks and joined the National Guard.

"I graduated from Alverno with $30,000 worth of loans, so I joined the National Guard to pay back my college tuition."

Marissa has truly risen above her past circumstances. Recently, she served as the director of the Second Harvest Food Bank and today is director of the Black Holocaust Museum in Milwaukee. When I spoke to her last year, she was getting ready to remarry.

"I paid my dues. There is a great sense of joy that follows sacrifice. If some things do not kill you, they ultimately make you stronger. I see coworkers cracking up over some minor thing on the job, and I want to say, 'Get over it, girl.'"

Another Alverno graduate, Debbie Sarnowski, had two children by the time she was twenty. Her ex-husband stayed home with the babies while she worked nights as a shift manager at McDonald's.

"For a while we were on welfare, too. I knew I didn't want to stay in that position. My parents influenced me to do whatever it took to get off welfare and get an education. Neither of them graduated from high school, but they both worked very hard in factories all their lives."

Like Marissa, Debbie had enormous obstacles to overcome before graduation. "My first husband was very abusive. After I left him, I went back to school. I was twenty-five years old at the time and had just gotten my driver's license. I arranged my entire schedule around my children. I worked at Alverno in the computer center. So many students at Alverno are mothers. We all helped each other with baby-sitting and study times. I could type school papers while I was doing my job, and my boss allowed me to pick up extra hours."

Debbie graduated from Alverno with a double major in business and communications. She has since remarried and has two more children.

"My husband and kids came to my graduation and cheered me on when I walked up on stage to receive my diploma. They all say they want to go to college, including the one with the learning disability."

There are seventy-four cousins in her family. She is only one of four in the history of her family who has ever graduated from college. Today, she is one of the top two Ameritech sales executives in the Milwaukee metro area.

"We are trying to save our money to buy a home and move out of here. Gangs are starting to rise up in our neighborhood. I know firsthand how important good role models are. My husband and I want to live someplace where our children are surrounded by good ones."

Alverno moms—Marissa and Debbie—remind me of a passage from Og Mandino's book, *The Spellbinder's Gift:* "Realize that almost every adversity that may befall you today usually carries with it an equivalent or greater benefit that you will find if you have the courage to look.

"Collect your thoughts whenever you suffer a setback and ask yourself what possible good can be extracted from your misfortune. . . . Never abandon hope. *Look for the seed of good in every adversity.*"

Lessons from Marissa and Debbie on overcoming obstacles are many.

Your past doesn't have to limit your future. Both of these women could have chosen to stay stuck in their family histories. Limited education. Abuse. Alcoholism. Welfare. It took courage to create a new future for themselves and their children.

They accomplished their goals by taking baby steps as they walked away from their past.

Focus on small, baby steps.

Ruth Harkin says, "If you think about your goals, they may sound impossible. Instead, you focus on one small step at a time. And you have to be extremely organized to keep things moving forward."

Marissa and Debbie first focused on passing the high school equivalency exam, although their ultimate goals were to get into college and then graduate.

The opposite of love is not hate but control. When Marissa was sixteen, it was sexy to have a boyfriend who got into fights with other guys who looked at her. But it's no fun when you are thirty or forty. Younger women are often fooled by the allure of possessiveness. I used to think it was cool when my steady went shopping with me to pick out a "dress that covers you."

This type of possessive behavior is a warning sign. If he is worried about your possible promiscuity, then he probably is already practicing it himself.

When the choice is either divorce or death, choose divorce. It helps if you start out possessing the maturity, knowledge, and common sense to make a good choice of marriage partners. But Marissa and Debbie did not. However, they recognized that divorce beats killing each other off.

Satisfaction ultimately does follow sacrifice. The Alverno moms made great sacrifices to get an education. They sacrificed being with their children and their children sacrificed being with their mom. But it was only temporary. Ultimately, their children are growing to be happier, healthier, and more educated than they would have been if Mom stayed on the dole.

Mother's Tough Love; A Daughter's Incredible Courage

Gail Harrington grew up with all the upper-middle-class advantages that Marissa and Debbie never had. Her mother was a nurse who became a stay-at-home mom. Her dad was a highly respected surgeon. Her parents fell in love when he was an intern and she was in nursing school. What obstacles could she have possibly overcome to merit being on this honor roll of hurdle-jumping moms?

"All the men in my family have doctorates. Education is important, and I graduated from college before I was twenty-one. I cannot say I was highly ambitious and career-oriented. I had a strong liberal arts background, and my primary interest was art history."

She saw herself having something to do with museums in between tending to husband and children. Married at twenty-two, she had two daughters by the time she was twenty-seven.

"At that age, you are very lucky if you pick the right person the first time."

The first three years after the girls were born, she designed, built, and decorated a beautiful new home. Her former husband was a successful entrepreneur.

"It was a beautiful home, but in a lot of ways it became meaningless to me. I came to see that we were two people with entirely different views of the world, merely coexisting in the same house. I was feeling like a slave in a country club prison: unnoticed, unappreciated, and doubting my own abilities. I decided to go back to work because the writing was on the wall and I didn't want to be one of those women who sits around crying and feeling helpless when the husband leaves."

She ended up taking a full-time job as an editorial assistant with a small publishing company.

"I didn't have a journalism degree, and not in my wildest dreams did I ever think I'd move up to become an editor. I took the job thinking it was a place to start, and the job fit my needs at the time. It was close to home and the hours were nine to five. It was a liberation, although it wasn't easy being a working mother of two active preschoolers."

It was a mutual separation with a successful fifty-fifty custody. However, her oldest daughter was their biggest challenge.

"Britany was a premature baby who rolled over for the first time in the nursery at the hospital. She had incredible energy. The nurses came in the first day and told me I was in for it. This was one determined human being."

Britany was climbing out of her crib at eight months and scaling the refrigerator at ten months. By the time she was a year old, they had to take the doorknob off the inside of Britany's room because she would climb out of the crib and go to the neighbor's house.

"The pediatrician kept reassuring me that things would calm down by the time she was three, but by age three, Britany had survived a rattlesnake bite and second-degree burns from pulling a pan of boiling water off a neighbor's stove. She was a happy kid with a great personality, but she was physically draining, especially to a full-time working mother. Fortunately, my younger daughter, Danika, was as easy as could be."

At age three, Britany was diagnosed with attention deficit disorder (ADD).

"Today, they have a lot more knowledge about ADD, but back then, schools didn't provide any special help for kids with ADD. Britany tested in the ninety-ninth percentile on standardized achievement tests, so the school considered her a smart kid with a behavior problem. It's difficult for ADD kids to function in a classroom with thirty-eight to forty other children, so they're often fooling around and getting into trouble.

"Getting into trouble became a way to get attention, and over time, these kids develop a bad self-image. As teenagers, they're more likely to get involved with drugs and alcohol."

By the time Gail had been promoted to managing editor of a national magazine, Britany was in junior high school, and her behavior and schoolwork were declining. It was clear that the problems were serious, and professional counseling was needed for all.

"When she was fourteen, Britany overdosed on antidepressants. The day afterward, I told my office I was leaving for lunch, but I really went to the hospital to see my daughter. She was lying there asleep, all hooked up to IVs. For a parent, that's a frightening sight. It felt like she was a breath away from death. Then she woke up and told me she was sorry and that she would never do anything like that again."

Ten days later, Britany was in an alcoholic coma.

Some parents give up on their kids. But Gail never lost sight of what a truly incredible daughter Britany was, constantly reminding her of those wonderful qualities she possessed.

"When it really got bad, I started learning what my options were. That gave me strength. I wasn't sitting at home, crying, and saying I could not take another day of this. I met with a counselor and researched various programs."

There were a series of hospitalizations and programs Britany participated in.

"When she was fourteen, I learned about an Outward Bound program in Maine, specifically for teenagers at risk. Britany was not happy about going. It was scary for both of us. I had to put her on a plane to Chicago and trust her to make her connecting flight. I wasn't sure she would show up."

But Britany arrived safely and stayed for a month of backpacking, canoeing, and climbing, giving her mother and sister a much-needed break.

"It wasn't a cure-all, but Britany learned many things about herself during that month that have stayed with her. She learned she could do things that were very hard to do when she pushed herself and stopped saying, 'I can't.'"

Britany still cherishes a photo from her Outward Bound program. The photo, taken during the rope-climbing course, shows Britany, the smallest and youngest in the group, leaning against the rock cliff face, crying as she hangs from the rope.

"I'm sure she was telling her leaders that she couldn't do it. She still keeps that photo in a frame on her desk as a wonderful reminder that she did go past her fear and make it to the top."

But shortly after she got back home, her sister Danika said, "She turned back into the teenager from Hell. The changes in her personality and drastic mood swings made her frightening to live with. I wanted her out of my life forever."

Gail continued to research the options.

"I heard about this residential treatment school in Utah. I knew I had to let go of her. She was on a mission of self-destruction, and I kept thinking I had to do something before it was too late.

"My younger daughter was so remarkable. She said to me one night when I was crying, 'Don't worry, Mom, we are going to make it. You are so strong. Other mothers would have killed themselves by now.'"

Britany went off screaming and kicking to Utah.

Was Gail feeling guilt-ridden?

As tough as Gail knew it would be for her daughter, she had no sympathy. "I had enough, and I was simply not qualified to help her. The school sent two staff workers down to accompany her to Utah. As she got into the car with them, she was crying and clutching a big brown stuffed gorilla. Her rebel-

> **No matter what, keep going and going and going.**

lious tough exterior had been reduced to what she really was: a scared little girl.

"But I was at peace because I knew Britany was going to be safe, and we could return to normalcy and have some good times together again."

Britany, a gifted writer like her mother, wrote this poem to her during those difficult days in Utah:

Lifestyles

Every day it gets a little harder.
And the reasons to cry are so easy to find.
Yet every day I get a little smarter.
Because I am leaving my old way of life behind.

When I think of the life I used to live
It often makes me cry for
This new lifestyle has so much more to give,
And that is why I am trying to say good-bye.

When I look back on the way that I treated you
I wonder why 'cause I needed you.
They say you hurt the ones you love the best,
And put the ones who don't deserve you above the rest.

Thank you for all the times you tried to help me out.
But understand it was only me I didn't care about.
I am sorry for all the anger I took out on you.
I had to want help first, now I have worked it through.

Still every day it gets a little harder.
And the reasons to cry are so easy to find.
Yet every day I get a little smarter.
Because I am leaving my old way of life behind.

And "The Brit" did. Today, she and her sister are hardworking college students. I wondered how Britany and her younger sister Danika's relationship weathered all the storms. Here's an excerpt from an essay that Danika (another wonderful writer) wrote about the person who had a significant influence in her life. She chose who else but her amazing and courageous sister, The Brit.

> *I suppose I learned a lot from Britany's mistakes and consequently avoided making the same ones, especially as a teenager. A lot of our family's energy and financial resources went to trying to help my sister, but she wasn't ready to be helped. When she was away in Utah for eighteen months, I felt like an only child, which was pretty fun.*
>
> *I became really active in sports and improved in school. I played soccer and basketball and worked twenty hours a week at Baskin Robbins, and it has taught me a lot about time management. Looking back, I realize that my sister is part of the reason I've made these commitments to positive activities and have been able to overcome some challenges.*
>
> *I believe that each of us has the power to be happy and successful and that we can't rely on others to make it happen for us. The fact that Britany finally discovered this and took charge of her life is further proof to me that all things are possible when we have goals.*
>
> *My sister is a miracle. And things between us are so different now. It has taken a lot of time for us to become sisters who are friends. Now, when she comes home from college to visit, we have a lot of fun hanging out together—but we always fight about who gets to ride shotgun with Mom.*

Gail says, "Sure, those were difficult years. Britany was so smart, and she looked like a cover girl for *Seventeen* magazine. Inside, she had so much pain. But even in the worst of times, there was a certain quality she had that made me believe she would make it. It wasn't always there, but every so often there was a flash from her—like a little light saying, 'The real me is still inside.'

"I think the three of us are all a lot stronger because of what we have been through together. There is a certain bond we have that is different from most parent-child relationships. We all are very proud of each other." On a separate piece of paper, list all the lessons Gail, Britany, and Danika taught you.

Don't Stop the Music

Pauline Kyne tap-danced her way into my life and this book. The first time I saw her was at a dance studio for little girls in Laguna Beach, California. I was signing up my then four-year-old daughter Kathleen for her tap and jazz classes. Pauline and her daughter Lisa's reputations as first-class dance teachers had preceded them. Lisa was the choreographer for the New York and Los Angeles productions of *Joseph and the Amazing Technicolor Coat*. All of us mothers felt blessed to have these two talented women instructing our daughters.

Pauline and Lisa's annual dance recitals featuring our children were as spectacular as anything you'd pay to go see on Broadway. The tickets to the performances are sold out fifteen minutes after they go on sale every spring. People from all over drive or fly down to see what the Kyne women are currently doing with all the little munchkins.

I'll never forget the first tap class I took Kath to. There were twelve four-year-old little squealing darlings that didn't know left from right. It was pure chaos. I said a silent prayer for Pauline as I exited the studio. When I returned to pick Kathleen up, a transformation had already taken place. These girls were in lines and counting the beats of the music. Four months later, any one of them could have been the star of *Annie* on Broadway.

When rehearsals started for Kath's first recital, I became very curious about the Kyne family. Lisa and her mother were co-directors and choreographers for the show, and I have never seen such mutual respect between human beings, much less a mother and a daughter. Then Lisa's dad Terry appeared on the scene, handling all the music and lighting. It was only later that I discovered Pauline and Terry had been divorced for many years, yet they acted like best friends.

"We are," she told me the day I interviewed her.

"Every day, I stop off at his apartment between classes and freshen up. We get along better now than we did during our twenty-year marriage. We were married when I was very young. He was a well-known director, and I was a regular on Canadian television variety shows. It was a very traditional marriage. And I just didn't seem to grow until after the fact. It's taken a lot of hard work to be where we are in this relationship. But I know our adult children—Lisa, Jenny, and Sean—are very happy we are."

They all celebrate holidays together, which sometimes includes significant others that are now in Pauline's or Terry's life. How did they make it through the pain?

"I started drinking when we moved to California. Before that, my career was going gangbusters in Canada."

Pauline had a spectacular television career that spanned from 1955 to 1970.

"I was the first woman choreographer in Canada. All my early dance training in England really paid off. I was probably the best all-around dancer. Tap, jazz, ballet, lots of musical theater. I got my equity card doing *The King and I* when I was twenty. Then I did CBC specials. I was a regular on the popular show, *The Hit Parade*."

Paul Anka did his famous number, "Oh, Diana," with Pauline. She also did big industrial shows for General Motors and other big companies. When she was nineteen, she met Terry on the set of a television show. They married in 1961 and had babies right away.

"But I kept dancing. I had a German nurse in the hospital who would come into my room and tell me, 'We will do our exercises now.' My German doctor knew I was a dancer, and he said it was important to stimulate the muscle as it heals."

Five weeks after Lisa was born, she was back dancing on television.

Meanwhile, Terry was fast becoming one of the best directors on television. Red Skelton offered him the director's job on his weekly show filmed in Los Angeles.

"He jumped at the opportunity. I wanted to go with him, but he felt it would be better to go first and feel the situation out. My parents, brothers, and sisters were all over in Canada by then. I was making big money, and it didn't seem practical to make the move just yet."

A year went by before Pauline and the kids made it to Los Angeles. By then, Terry had a new and exciting life.

"I wasn't really a part of it. I was home all day with the kids. I had nothing else going. Terry never minded me working, but he expected me to find the help. That was a problem for me in California. I had family in Canada, but I had no one to turn to in L.A. That's when I started drinking. I wasn't about to go audition and leave my kids with just anybody. Plus I had one horrible experience. I went to audition and left them with a sitter who I later found out was one of the Charles Manson gang. It terrified me. Terry said, 'Well, if you can't find a sitter, then you can't go to work.'"

By then, Lisa was heavy into dance lessons and the other two were busy with their activities.

"I was home alone a lot, and I'd drink wine. I don't think I realized how wrenching leaving my career would be for me. I left Canada when I was really in demand and at my peak. I felt so trapped in Los Angeles."

At five o'clock every afternoon, Pauline would pour her first glass of wine.

"It started escalating. Two glasses, then three. I used to put myself in this wonderful dream state. I would imagine I was dancing and play games with myself. I'd choreograph spectacular dance routines in my head."

The children didn't know she was drinking because she wouldn't pour the second glass until they were in bed. Eventually, fourteen-year-old Lisa caught on.

"When it started interfering with my kids, I think I started to wake up. I was a different person when I drank. Angry, cried a lot, no motivation. A friend insisted I go to AA, and I was belligerent there, too, telling everybody at the meetings I was not like the rest of them. I only drank a little wine."

Pauline's AA friends helped her see the light, and she eventually jumped on the wagon.

"I figured when I stopped drinking, my marriage would straighten out. But it was too late. By then, there was someone else in Terry's life, and we had grown far too distant."

There were years of anger over other women and regrets about giving up her own successful career, but Pauline has put that all behind her now.

"What I didn't gain in fame and fortune in Canada, I made up for in gut living in the States. My personal growth and the tremendous relationship I have with Terry and our children today far surpasses any ambitions I ever had."

Pauline's new career isn't too shabby, either. The Kyne Dance Academy is one of the best in the country. Lisa and Pauline's all-girl dance group called the Groove Team are cleaning up at all the national dance contests. Mothers by the carload continue to celebrate Pauline's presence.

Researcher Deborah Carr of the University of Wisconsin reported, "Job goals play what some might see as a surprisingly large part in a midlife woman's well-being."

Her findings come from an ongoing study of 3,052 women that originated at their high school graduations in 1957. They were surveyed again at ages thirty-five and fifty-three.

"Compared with women who attained their goals, those who fell short had lower levels of psychological well-being and higher levels of depression. They also reported less sense of a purpose in life.

"Not having a work goal predicts bad news, too: Women with no future goal at thirty-five had poorer mental health by fifty-three than those who did, even when their depression level before thirty-five was taken into account."

Lessons from Pauline Kyne:

A woman's passion and vocation is the key to her well-being. "My children knew how important it was for me to dance. My drinking was a cry and plea to anybody: Please don't stop my music."

The most dangerous human weakness: Denial. "I thought the amount of booze I drank was what separated me from the rest of the people at AA. I found out it was the amount of courage that they had, which I didn't possess yet, that truly separated us."

ALL THE KING'S HORSES AND ALL THE KING'S MEN

Tomazina Mulhearn was living the good life. She and her partner/husband Bruce owned and managed thirty of the most successful real estate offices in southern California. They had the perfect family, two healthy and very bright children and just what they ordered, too—one boy and one girl.

"Bruce thought our baby days were over. But nine years after our son Kurt was born, I found out I was pregnant again. I was thirty-six. We were just beginning to travel and kick up our heels. The fruits of ours labor were starting to pay off big time."

"Our third child, Sean, was born right on time and the picture of health. He possessed the same happy-go-lucky personality that his brother and sister did."

Then one morning, Tomazina took Sean for his well-baby checkup. And from that day forward, their family life would never be the same again.

"There was nothing unusual going on. Sean was just getting his first DPT shot. But shortly after I brought him home, he started tremoring uncontrollably on the right side of his body. All his muscular features dropped. He couldn't lift his head."

Tomazina rushed him to the closest hospital.

"They told me there was nothing they could do, suggesting I could watch him at home just as easily as at the hospital. So we went back home, and for the next five hours I held him tight through what I didn't realize at the time was a kind of seizure—the petit mal."

It was the first of thousands of petit mals Sean would go through over the next twenty-four years.

"After that night, he was never the same again. We didn't connect up all the seizures with having the inoculations. So when it was time for his second DPT we took him for another one. The seizures continued to get worse, and the doctors kept prescribing very strong medication."

Seven years later, a new doctor identified the problem.

"He directed me to go home and check when Sean had his first bad seizure which, of course, was after he received his first DPT shot. Don't ask me why none of us realized the coincidence."

By the time Sean was three, he was severely retarded. His seizures were like clockwork—fifteen minutes every morning. "And they continued all day. His physical development was fine, but mentally, he stayed at the toddler level. Bright lights of any type triggered the seizures, so we needed to keep him in dark rooms. But he was always trying to escape out of the house. He despised the dark."

They had him tested at UCLA. The doctor said anything could happen. Sean could end up snapping out of it and be fine or get worse with each seizure. The doctor told Tomazina the best thing she could do was to spend as much time as she could afford just talking to Sean and reading to him.

"So that is what I did. I was pulled away from an exciting life. My life centered around Sean and the four walls for the next twelve years."

By the time he was seven years old, he was having tremendous bouts of anxiety, throwing tantrums, and running away constantly. He was heavily medicated due to the seizures.

"This was a very happy child who must have wondered what the heck happened to him. He was so frustrated. Gritting his teeth, screaming at the top of his lungs. Plus he had enormous physical strength."

When Sean was twelve years old, Tomazina knew she needed to cut the cord. They were together night and day, and she was looking for a break. Sean needed to get more schooling and discover relationships with other caregivers. She went back to their real estate company for part of the day, enlisted the aid of an in-house helper, and sent Sean to a school for the retarded for part of the day.

Sean is now twenty-four and has never been institutionalized.

"People talk about human potential. When I went through this nightmare with Sean, I wondered what God wanted from me. What potential would I not be developing because of sacrifices I needed to make to be with him?

"Eventually, I understood that Sean's handicap taught every member of our family how to become unconditional lovers. Isn't our most important mission on earth to discover our potential for love?

"We were so focused on material goals, so caught up in the world, when Sean's seizures hit."

Lessons from Tomazina:

Stay open and willing, and the angels will come to help. "At first, I was wrapped up in resentment. Why me? Why Sean? Then I met a woman who had three handicapped sons and no money. We were so fortunate to be able to take care of our boy. But this woman who had nothing did something incredible. She opened up a home for retarded boys—sixteen of them—in Ojai, California, so she could be with her three sons. She refused to wrap herself up in self-pity, and the angels came into her life. They've come to our house, too. It's been a gradual molding, knowing how to do our best for Sean. But this discovery has become our spiritual training ground."

When all else fails, look for the humor in every situation. "Sean is a true character. He's always having a good time, a real comedian. But he's also extremely independent and at times very stubborn. Sometimes I want to wring his neck, but I am laughing so hard I don't have the strength. This particular day was one of those times.

"That morning, and many other mornings, Sean insisted on dressing himself. That day he put on plaid bermuda shorts, the kind the retirees down in Florida wear when they play golf. His Mickey Mouse shirt, his favorite brown corduroy sport jacket that is two sizes too small, red knee-high Christmas socks that played 'Jingle Bells' every time he took a step and pressed hard on his heel. He was happier than a clam when he got into the front seat of my car to go run errands with me.

"So we were merrily driving down the freeway in my station wagon and Sean, who loves music, was singing "C'monna-to-my house" along with Rosemary Clooney. I was looking straight ahead, and the windows were up with the tape blasting, so I was not paying any attention to drivers trying to signal me that my car was smoking.

"Finally, I saw sparks flying, and I pulled off to the side of the freeway. The car was starting to go up in flames, and I couldn't get Sean's door open because it was so close to the guardrail. Which meant I had to go on the freeway side of the car and pull him out myself. He was furious with me because he wanted to get out by himself, so he resisted my effort to move him toward me. And he's a very strong guy."

Tomazina says at that point, a shot of mother's emergency adrenaline pumped through her veins, and she grabbed his ankles and literally dragged him out of the burning car.

"He was roaring mad. Could've cared less about going up in flames. He was upset because I wouldn't let him get out of the car on his own. So he jumped out in the middle of the freeway, with cars whizzing past, and he would not come back, no matter how hard I pleaded.

"I didn't know what to do. People drove up with extinguishers. Someone else started working on my car. Someone else called the fire department. And I was still walking out in the middle of the freeway, dodging cars, and trying to coax this kid back to me."

Then she spotted the phone about twenty paces behind her.

"I walked over to the phone and yelled to Sean, 'Somebody wants to talk to you, Sean. Do you want to take this phone call?'"

Sean loves to talk on the phone, so she hit his hot button.

"And that is how I finally got him out of harm's way. But then the police and fire department came, and they wanted us out of there, but Sean wouldn't get off the phone. Plus he was getting all this attention from police and firemen. He was laughing to beat the band. At one point, the police thought they could strong-arm him, but no way.

"Then, out of the blue, a female sheriff pulled up. She knew just how to handle this joker. She drove up, surveyed the situation, turned on her loudspeaker, and called Sean's name, asking him if he was interested in talking on her speaker.

"He walked over to her car like a little puppy dog, opened the door, got in, started yapping, and off they drove."

Patience. Tomazina says Sean teaches her how to be patient every day. "This is a virtue you carry into every part of your life."

A bigger capacity to reach out to others instead of stand by and judge them. "I look at the world so differently now. You learn not to condemn or pass judgment. The change in your soul reflects the change in your character and your outward actions. We all want to get rid of pain. We want to go down easy street. But you never get to discover your true human potential if you live on easy street."

Tomazina, Betty, Kelly, Pauline, Gail and Britany, Debbie, and Marissa inspire and motivate me. Each of them remind us that we learn more from failure than we do from success.

It is my prayer that the sharing of such personal accounts of other mothers' trials will inspire each of us to never give up. Such true grit stories restore our sense of hope and energize us to move onward and upward. And yes, together, we shall overcome.

CHAPTER SEVEN

Makeovers

A mother's life is a continuous act of faith. From the moment of conception through labor and delivery, we literally fly blind into the most important role of our life: motherhood. Those first nine months, we have no idea what is going to happen to our bodies or when our babies will, if ever, arrive.

Sure, doctors do predict delivery dates, but all six of my children's arrival times were off by four weeks. My faith was tested to the limits of my strength, especially with my firstborn. Once the second week of the predicted date passed, I seriously doubted whether my pregnancy would ever end. I even doubted certain parts of my body still existed—like my feet.

Once the baby comes into the world, this new little life is a complete mystery to us. Slowly, we learn who this individual is, but this person keeps changing. It takes enormous faith to believe that he or she will make it into adulthood.

Gail Harrington is the perfect example of faith in action. She kept flying blind with Britany through her drug problems when neither of them could see the light at the end of the tunnel.

When our children grow into adulthood, we have to renew our faith in them almost daily as they make their own hard choices. For me, this time of their lives has tested my faith in them much more than when they were learning to ride a bike or take a first step.

Faith is your formula for receiving the magic makeover.

Mothers learn firsthand that faith is the magic formula for the ultimate makeover.

BEAUTY AND THE BEAST

The ultimate makeover means a personal transformation. No matter how many times I go see *Beauty and the Beast*, I always come away spiritually moved. We are all part Beauty and part Beast. The Beast is our weaker, selfish aspect. Because we are human, we are susceptible to such weakness. But our true destiny on earth is to grow the Beauty side of ourselves—that very simple self who shows us how to attain true happiness and peace of mind. I bet even Mother Teresa had been plagued by the Beast. And I bet her great compassion and love of the human race grew as she honestly and painfully confronted that darker side of herself.

I found that the challenge of successfully balancing career and family became so much easier a task for me as I began spending less and less time at war with the Beast. I think of this ungodly monster as my ego—the darker side of myself I am trying to destroy. This execution process is called "ego-slaying," and its no walk in the park. It's painful and it takes awhile.

The rewards of ego-slaying, in terms of my overall well-being, far exceed the pain of execution. I think you will find if you apply the principles of ego-slaying offered in this chapter, what you once considered a demanding life will become your greatest source of peace, joy, and satisfaction.

Think of this spiritual exercise as nondenominational. People of all races, color, and gender can expect positive results from this execution. So how does one go about slaying the ego?

EGO-SLAYING

Is there some kind of easy ego-exorcism one can self-administer to kill off this monster once and for all? That's like asking if there is a way you can become a mother without going through labor and delivery. There is no escaping the procedure. But, like childbirth, ego-slaying classes are plentiful. The classroom is our life, and our teachers can be found everywhere we look.

Grow your beauty and slay your beast (ego).

I was first introduced to the challenging task of ego-slaying about thirty years ago while reading Catherine Marshall's book *Beyond Ourselves*. She devoted a whole chapter to the subject. It's embarrassing to think of how many times I've had to reread it. The beastly ego truly loves to rear its ugly head without prior notice.

In her book she describes how much of her spiritual journey was centered around battling with her ego. She discovered during a retreat in the mountains with some of her other Christian friends that they were having the same ego problems that she was.

Marshall and her friends came to the following conclusion: "There is no maturity or fulfillment of man's [woman's] personality—apart from the slaying of egocentricity."

By the close of the retreat, they had worked out a plan for slaying the ego.

1. We see the limitation of self-centered living and the danger of it in every area of our life.

2. We pass sentence on the natural self by telling God that we are willing to have Him slay it. Our statement of willingness is a definite act at a given time.

3. We accept by faith the fact that God has heard us; that the next action will be His. We reckon by faith that He has indeed undertaken the execution.

4. There will be a crisis or a series of crises. We live through them step by step. This is the overt evidence that the slaying of the self has been undertaken.

5. Every day of our lives we shall still have to choose between selfishness and unselfishness. But the big decision to let God rather than self rule makes all the smaller decisions easier.

All seven members of that group agreed to these five points, and all seven of them were tested in different ways over the following weeks. "We each discovered that the 'execution of the self' is the greatest crisis," Marshall wrote.

For me, ego-slaying has become an ongoing process in my life. I find that when I am more willing to cooperate with the process, it ends sooner and is less painful.

Part of the process of ego-slaying is being aware. I have to be able to take ownership of my shortcomings. Until I am willing to do that, no ego-slaying will take place.

For example, a downfall of mine is being preoccupied with outcomes—a pastime of the ego. Maybe it's because I grew up on fairy tales or in an outcome-oriented society. Remember, I am the one who cut pictures of Jane Fonda out of a magazine and hung them on my refrigerator. I once pinned a poster of snow skiers heading down a mountain on my office wall, hoping to make enough sales to take our family on a Christmas ski trip.

Nothing is particularly wrong with wanting to travel to nice places or have a fit body. But once the good intention comes to mind, it is much more productive during the process of accomplishing the goal to be able to forget about reaching the goal. If you don't learn how to put a desired goal on the back burner of your mind while trying to attain it, the goal will either elude you or take twice the time to achieve it.

It is critical that we forget thinking about the goal. The strength to reach the goal never comes from thinking about the outcome. Thinking about the outcome actually pushes it farther away from our reach. Here is the perfect example of how I have expended negative energy, thanks to the ego, worrying about an outcome.

Remember to forget about outcomes.

After I transcribed all the interviews for this book, I stared at the foot-high stack of papers on my desk and said to myself, I can't write this book. It's way out of my league. Who died and crowned you queen of all mothers? Nobody is going to spend ten cents to buy this book.

What was I going to get out of this whole writing effort, anyway? Fame? Fortune?

It was that beastly control freak in me rearing its ugly head and demanding answers and hating delayed gratification.

Self-doubt, the ego's companion, always seems to creep up on me when the pressure is on and the goal is at hand.

So, as I felt those familiar black clouds of uncertainty starting to temporarily darken my disposition, I exorcized such evil spirits by immediately applying the five steps of ego-slaying. The first step is an awareness of the danger of self-centered living. Concentrating on outcomes is a symptom of self-centered living. I knew I was in trouble.

I purposely did something that symbolically put no importance on the mood I was in. I turned up Neil Diamond singing "I've been this way before. I'll be this way again." And then I repeated the words, "This, too, shall pass," while proceeding as planned, no matter how I felt.

I paid attention to my beautiful side, the side that frankly doesn't give a damn about the outcome. My beautiful side thought about how my cup has already runneth over during the process of interviewing and writing. I then reminded myself that writing this book gave me the opportunity to meet some fine women. During our brief meetings, each one of them allowed me to share their experiences vicariously—experiences that never would have become a part of my life without our meeting one another.

So all I really needed to do was to just sit back and recall those feelings and experiences. And then shut up and write. Easier said than done, of course. It took plenty of extra effort to stay on track. The source of the problem? I repeat: The ego, demanding to know the outcome.

All of us moms are working on ego-slaying. Years ago, Dr. Marel Hanks committed to a goal to begin medical school once her children were well established in grade school. In that profession she did not have the option of studying to be a doctor on a part-time basis.

Her only option was to make her move when she felt the time was right. She seriously committed to that goal a few years before she was able to act on it: She would begin medical school in her early thirties when her children were in a certain grade. It was a done deal. All she needed to do was patiently wait until the designated time. She needed to have faith and trust in herself that her goal would happen.

Meanwhile, she needed to enjoy the time with her little children.

"My only regret is that I did not appreciate that time at home with my children before I started medical school. I could have if I had been more trusting. Instead of trusting that it was going to happen, instead of just sitting back and relaxing and enjoying where I was at that time of my life with my kids, I kept doubting myself. I kept wishing the time would pass more quickly. There was this terrible sense of urgency going on inside me."

Sound familiar? The ego hates the present moment. The ego trusts nothing. Think of your ego as a demanding, spoiled child who refuses to learn how to delay gratification. The ego will stop at nothing when it comes to tormenting us. The ego is the true source of the stress and anxiety that comes into our lives. We bring on our own problems by giving in to the demands of the ego.

Valerie Menges says her ego was responsible for making her paranoid and guilt-ridden. "When our nine-month-old daughter died, I blamed myself. I always felt that if I had left work a few hours earlier and taken her to the hospital, instead of waiting for her scheduled afternoon doctor's appointment, perhaps she wouldn't have died. These feelings spilled over into the relationship I had with my husband, too. I convinced myself that he also was blaming me for not taking her to the doctor sooner. Of course, he never said such a thing to me."

Valerie brought these feelings up during a talk with her spiritual advisor and pastor.

"We prayed about my feelings and discussed the situation. He asked me if there was the proper medicine or medical procedures available at the time that could have saved our daughter. It was common knowledge that such procedures did not exist then.

"What was truly amazing was the discussion I had with my husband following the talk I had with my pastor. I told him I thought he was secretly blaming me for the death of our daughter and that he felt, because I worked, I was not a good mother."

Her husband told her that such thoughts never occurred to him. He deeply loved her and felt they did everything humanly possible at that time to help their daughter.

Egos are control freaks. Even when circumstances go way beyond human control, our egos try to convince us that we have the supreme power over life and death. No wonder

Valerie felt so guilty. Never mind that the proper medical attention was not available during that period of time for her daughter's disease.

Valerie's ego convinced her that she controlled her child's destiny. And Valerie's ego convinced her that her husband also thought she had that power, and that he, too, blamed her for not keeping his daughter alive.

"I had carried the burden of my own guilt for so long, and it was such a relief to let it go."

Valerie's situation made me think once again about the part guilt plays in the working mother's life. In the first chapter, I said guilt was often a healthy feeling the conscience manifests to help us parents do the right thing. But all feelings, if left unchecked, have the power to help the ego take control and seriously distort our thinking.

Valerie's guilt turned to shame. No one doubts that she would have taken her daughter to the doctor's office sooner if she knew it was a life or death situation. She made the best move at the time, based on the information she had. But the ego trusts no one. In her vulnerable state of mind, Valerie's ego turned her guilt to all-out shame.

Terry Savage's ego kept her pushing too hard and too long career wise. "My kidneys shut down, but I paid no attention. I had convinced myself that the stock market and my customers wouldn't make it without me."

Shirley Pepys's ego kept her jumping through hoops to please people until she felt completely unloved and unappreciated.

Candice Copeland Brooks's ego had her convinced for a while to say yes to jobs that she not only did not want to take on but that she resented because the work kept her away from her children.

Pauline Kyne said her ego convinced her she was "a better person than most of those losers who went to AA meetings. I did not think I drank to the degree they did. I was different."

The ego never needs anybody's help. Single-handedly, it can take us down into the deepest and darkest bowels of life.

Some people think believing in God or belonging to a certain religion is humanity's way of shielding ourselves from the reality of death. Perhaps that is true. But on the other hand, could that be the ego trying to convince us not to buy into faith and religion?

After all, the ego thinks it's all-knowing and in total control of all outcomes. On the contrary, faith means believing in the unknown and taking comfort in not knowing and not having to worry about the outcome. It's letting go of ourselves in order to truly enjoy the present. Faith is in total opposition to the ego. The ego uses our own anger and bitterness to keep us clinging to the past. Faith uses forgiveness and reconciliation to resurrect us to a new and better future.

> **Faith uses forgiveness and reconciliation to strengthen you.**

From Human to Divine

This book is full of answers. Answers that were discovered through the trial and error of balancing family and career. But every mother knows there are some problems that have no answers. Only time, reflection, and a faith in life can heal. When a family suddenly suffers the death of a child, a divorce, money dilemmas, or delinquency issues, nothing seems to make sense. Many years later when we look back on those difficult seasons of our lives, we know that nothing human supported our strength at those times. It's as if we became superhuman temporarily and coped with the trial. I think of the mother or father who upon seeing their child pinned under the bottom of a truck instinctively have the strength to lift the danger away. Something out of the ordinary fuels us. I like to think of those times as our divine moments.

But once the crisis passes, the divine adrenaline can diminish. So I have found it important in my life to create a space for more opportunities that allow the divine to grow. Not just in moments of extreme joy or crisis. I want to be able to see the divine in ordinary times. And when we see the divine in the human, we are full of joy and so grateful. And not near as grouchy! Because it is as if we put on a new pair of glasses. This new vision cannot happen by accident. We have to look for a window of opportunity each day to reflect on what is important in the midst of this demanding existence. The makeover—the evolution of becoming more compassionate and human as we grow in life—is only possible when we make reflection and quiet time a priority.

So how does faith or religion figure into finding the divine? Does it help or hinder our makeover and desire to become more loving? (Isn't that what life is all about?)

Faith is the dance and religion is the style.

Faith is the dance. Religion is the style. You and I may both have faith. You may be Muslim, I may be Catholic, your best friends might be Jewish, or your coworkers might be Hindu. The religion part of it is only the outward expression of faith. But like dancers, the faithful have the option of choosing many ways to express their faith through their membership in certain religions.

My religion was handed down to me from my two sets of grandparents. The Dolces, my mother's parents, who immigrated to America from Italy, and the Barretts, my father's parents, who also came over on the boat but from Ireland.

I was baptized Catholic when I was a baby and grew up in the Catholic religion. My parents went to daily Mass. I attended Catholic schools for sixteen years. But I truly didn't understand what a treasured gift had been handed down to me until I went through a crisis of faith.

After I divorced my first husband and my friend committed suicide, I stopped going to church. That wouldn't have been so bad, but I also temporarily lost my faith. That was a decision I made in cooperation with my ego.

I was angry at the Catholic church because I could no longer go to communion because of my divorce. I didn't understand how the church could allow annulments yet condemn divorce. And my parish priest seemed like a righteous, old-school Irishman. Obviously, my ego was ruling the roost during that era of my life.

My career and children continued to grow and prosper, but I felt restless and separated from some part of myself. For a while, I attended churches of other denominations, but I missed the liturgy: the Mass, receiving the Eucharist, and the Sacrament of Reconciliation. These were rituals, like certain dances, that I've drawn great satisfaction and comfort from over the years. For some folks, the Mass may seem like a lot of hocus-pocus. Confession may be a trip to the guilt box, but in my life, the sacraments had become great sources of internal healing.

A few years after my friend died, I went back to my college alma mater to give a speech. While I was there, I spent time visiting a nun who was my drama teacher and spiritual mentor in college. She had remained one of my most trusted friends and confidantes throughout the years.

I told Sister Xavier that I hadn't been to Mass for a long time. I also shared my disillusionment with organized religion. But I told her I felt a void. Something was missing. By then, I was very much in love with Mike, and we were soon to be married. I will never forget what she told me. I've paraphrased her words here: "You now have the family you always wanted. I know your career brings you a great deal of satisfaction, too. You were always one who needed to have many irons in the fire. So, for what may be stressful for another woman, for you is energizing and fulfilling.

"But I know you too well, Danielle. You have a faith that was handed down to you from your ancestors that you hold dear. There is an emptiness in your life that a man, all the children a home can hold, or all the money in the bank will not be able to satisfy within you."

I broke down and cried in her arms. I knew she was right. Shortly after our visit, I started to pray again. Then, slowly but surely, I was back attending Mass and celebrating the beautiful rituals of my faith. My visit with Sister Xavier happened over twenty years ago.

Since that time, both my husband and I have reconciled with and renewed our commitment to the church. As important as it was for us to proceed with these outward formalities of religion, the real joy comes from once again being able to access meaningful tradition and ritual together with a community of believers who all have the same goal to express our faith and gratitude to our Creator.

Candice Copeland Brooks drifted away from her church for a while, too. "I grew up in a certain religion, but during my young adulthood I drifted away for a while. A few years before I got married, I felt a hole—a void in my life. Then I asked myself what was missing."

She and her husband Doug started attending their church regularly again. "We renewed ourselves spiritually, and because we did, every aspect of our life improved. I think motherhood escalated my spiritual need even more. When I got pregnant, I realized I was no longer in control."

Pray over all your choices and decisions.

Churchgoing or participating in rituals is not the only way to express one's faith. Tom and Ruth Harkin are not "active in any churches, and we sometimes do not get to church on Sunday," but they have instilled in their children a strong faith.

Tom said, "We've taught them to always question who we are and why we are here, to ask what is bigger than ourselves. None of what we see in creation could have happened without some grand design or superior being. You can hear from all these different religions, and they can tell you who God is and how He operates and how He thinks, but the only person who can discover God is you."

People

Marissa Cobb Weaver discovered that other believers in her community helped her discover and strengthen her faith. "I couldn't relate to so-called Christians. On the surface, it seems they have these perfect little lives. None of them seemed to have crises. I had to search for people who struggled like me. I found them and asked them how they kept their faith in the midst of struggle. They taught me how to personalize God."

Crises and Unexplainable Events

Joanne Konz said it took a while to make spirituality and the strengthening of her faith a priority in her life, but now it's her anchor point. "I know people survive without it, and are very happy, but for me, it is extremely important. I began realizing a spiritual life after my thirty-two-year-old brother died. And then my dad passed away shortly after that. I still feel a close spiritual connection with them.

"When we were kids growing up, the first one to see a robin in springtime got a dime from Dad. But all of us always got one because Dad usually saw the first robin. Then he would call us all outside to look at the one he spotted.

"Springtime, about five years ago and shortly after my father passed away, I saw a robin on the side of the road. I whispered to myself, 'Dad, you owe me a dime.'"

While showering the following morning, Joanne looked down and saw a dime at her feet.

"Since then, dimes keep showing up in strange places. When we were looking for a sitter to take care of the children, a woman named Betty answered an ad we ran in the paper. She was in her fifties and older than the other sitters I normally used, which bothered me a little.

"After she worked three days for us, I asked her to spend the night because I wanted to get to know her and see if I would feel better about her being with the children. After she went upstairs to go to bed, I called up to her, asking if there was anything she needed. She yelled down, 'No, but thanks for the dime.'

"I yelled back, 'Pardon me?' And that's when she told me there was a dime sitting in the middle of her bed when she pulled back the covers. I had goose bumps. Then I thought to myself, 'Dad is telling me it is okay.' And Betty truly turned out to be a godsend." Or should we call her a Dad-send?

Paula Perry believes she and her husband Keith would not be the proud parents of their two adopted children today if certain events had not occurred in their life.

"We were living in Phoenix. I was a nurse and Keith was remodeling homes. The hustle and bustle of city life was wearing on us. Plus we had been trying to have children to no avail. We wanted to change our lifestyle. Leave the city and find work we could do together because we had compatible skills."

The Perrys researched small towns, ultimately ending up in one in Idaho. They opened a restaurant, and a couple who came into their restaurant led them down the path to parenthood.

"They were steady customers, and they had just adopted a baby, and they heard we wanted to adopt. We ended up going over to their house and finding out about the procedures.

"For faith to make a difference, you have to tune in and listen like you would tune in and listen to a radio. Then you have to trust that an answer will come. In our case, the answer came through the couple who walked into the restaurant. They appeared right in front of our faces. We were directed to this town and this business. In Arizona, the waiting time to adopt a child was seventeen years. Our entire life would have been totally different. This path, which required us to have so much faith, has turned out to be a real blessing."

Let go.

Finding Silence

More than anything I value silence. It took time to become comfortable with silence. And when I finally let myself discover my quiet time, the sounds and activity of my life became more authentic and enjoyable. My quiet time consists of reflection, meditation and, other times, prayer. Since childhood my Catholic beliefs have led me to a discovery of prayer. But it doesn't really matter what your beliefs are. It's true Buddhism, Judaism, Hinduism, and others support a form of quiet time or prayer. But even if you do not have a set of religious beliefs, you need the comfort of silence.

A dear friend of mine who happens to be my yoga instructor conducts a marvelous class that combines yoga with chanting. She has a beautiful and soothing voice. And she begins each class with a different spontaneous mantra that surfaces from her soul. I always leave her class refreshed and thankful for the yoga movement, silence, and chanting. What a combination. Following that movement and reflection time, my whole day takes on a new and grateful energy.

My quiet time has led me to a more authentic life. When I am alone and honestly quiet, I cannot escape from myself or hide from the truth.

A few years ago, I presented a three-day sales clinic. The preparation for this workshop was very demanding. My husband and I hired telemarketers to sell tickets. Four weeks before the program, very few tickets had been sold. At the time,

I was writing a book and giving about five speeches a month around the country. Because of no ticket sales, it was necessary for me to go out and sell tickets to companies with sales forces on those days when I was not out of town.

Fly blind.

It's fun.

This took time away from my family, especially Kathleen, who was only five years old. I spent the last six weeks before the workshop doing three presentations a day at various companies in and around our county. I was able to sell enough tickets to fill up the hotel room, but in the process, I had turned into Oscar the Grouch.

The program was successful and everyone who participated asked me to repeat it the following year. I knew firsthand what a repeat performance would involve. The venture was profitable, and the next one had the potential of being even more so. But as I prayed, I realized I had paid a high price for the profits made—an emotional distance from my husband and daughter that took a while to repair.

When we use ego-slaying and silence to help transform us from beast to beauty, we no longer measure the success of an undertaking in terms of dollars and cents or strictly material perks. We measure our success in terms of invisible considerations. Are we less or more loving because of this experience? Less or more compassionate? Patient? These are the permanent rewards that ultimately will lead us to more peace and even material prosperity than one could ever imagine.

I pray before every speech. I pray each morning before I type one word on my screen. It's always the same prayer: "I am an instrument in Your hands. Use me your way, not mine."

More than anything, making my spirituality a priority is responsible for making me a more confident wife and mother. Learning more about your spiritual side (the quiet, reflective you) can work miracles in your life. Here are some of the best approaches to developing your spiritual muscle that I have discovered.

Be silent. Learn to love silence. Look for a block of time every day when you can just be quiet. Be still. Make this your time of reflection.

Mother Teresa wrote:

The fruit of Silence is Prayer
The fruit of Prayer is Faith
The fruit of Faith is Love
The fruit of Love is Service
The fruit of Service is Peace.

So it all begins with silence, doesn't it?

Candice and Doug Brooks often take silent hikes up into the mountains, "silently looking and listening at nature. It's a spiritual experience. The wildflowers, the birds, the crevices in the mountains formed over hundreds of years. No words are needed. The awestruck feelings of thanksgiving and gratitude form the prayer."

Besides planning daily times of silence, I've gotten into the habit of going away once a year to make silent retreats. Author Diane de Dubovay says it's a journey "not so much to a place as a state of mind."

> **Be silent at least fifteen minutes a day.**

Every time I check into a retreat house, I know that I will come away with a whole new realization about my life. Some years I've retreated with one goal in mind: to be healed. The emotional hangovers suffered from divorce, death, career disappointments, and harsh confrontations with family and friends can take its toll on our lives.

Withdrawing from the world and cloistering ourselves in a protected sanctuary, where prayer, meditation, and spiritual counseling are the priorities of the day, becomes as important to the health of a soul as time spent at a spa can be for the tired and aching body.

Other years, I've retreated to simply say thank you and celebrate the blessings received during the past year. Regardless of your religious orientation, here are some of my favorite retreat spots (and you do not have to be Catholic to visit):

> Mary and Joseph Retreat House
> Palos Verdes, California
>
> The Franciscan Retreat Center
> Scottsdale, Arizona
>
> The Serra Retreat House
> Malibu, California
>
> St. Andrew's Priory
> Valyermo, California

There are plenty of good resources for finding a retreat house that will suit you: the bulletin board at New Age bookstores, the Catholic Archdiocese offices in any city, yoga centers, Zen Buddhist temples, night school, and college education catalogues. Wilderness retreats are available through the Sierra Club.

I've always walked away from a retreat feeling deeply refreshed and ready to confront my everyday world with a renewed understanding of both myself and the people who live with me in that world. If silence is not your thing, you'll discover why it should be at the end of a retreat.

Find a secret spot to pray. *Go to a convenient place.* Find a place of quiet reflection where you can go to every day. If praying is new for you, having this place to withdraw silently into yourself for fifteen minutes or so helps get you started. In no time, you will learn how to withdraw into yourself and pray anywhere.

A working mother I know who is vice president of an international sales company travels frequently. Fifteen years ago, she got into the habit of practicing prayer meditation whenever she boarded a plane. As soon as her airplane reaches cruising altitudes, she meditates for thirty minutes.

"When I am home, I do it at a local park that I pass on the way to work in the morning. I attribute both my peaceful family life and the steady, upward progression of my career to my prayer life. As I explore my interior life, asking myself questions such as, Who am I? Where do I come from? Why am I here?, the right decisions in the material world become blatantly clear."

Select your place of quiet and reflection. It can be a park, a beach alongside the ocean or lake, a special room in your house, or a church. Our church is open all day. I love to go make a visit and light a candle.

Wherever you choose, make sure it feels like home. Sit in a comfortable position. Don't worry about having to kneel on a concrete floor or in a wooden pew in order to make your quiet time more effective. You can walk along the beach, a river, or a seldom-traveled country road. The important thing is that it becomes your place to be still in your form of reflection.

Become aware. Once you go to your reflection spot, sit back and relax. Clear your mind. Stop dwelling on the problems and concerns of the day. Concentrate on your breathing or initiate Kathy Smith's BLT technique in Chapter 4. It can help you to get into the present moment. Richard Odom's meditation may help: "Breathe in, silently saying, 'My body is strong.'"

Once you are focused and feeling calm, reflect on the events of your day. The purpose of this quiet reflection is to sharpen your sense of observation. For example, last Christmas, when all my children came up for the holidays, there was initially confusion. The son who was in the accident had surgery a few days prior to his arrival. He was taking pain medication.

Everyone was tense, which resulted from the travel time to get here. I was very concerned about the preparation of all the holiday meals. In general, we were all a pretty sensitive, jumpy bunch. During my daily meditation, I reflected on each one of my children by sharply bringing into focus their individual faces.

At one point, while observing my son who had just come through jaw surgery, I noticed his eyes. Fearful ones with dark circles underneath. I was overwhelmed with sadness and began to cry. For an instant, I felt his pain and the terrible shock of his accident.

I had been telling him how lucky he was. It was only during my daily prayer that I finally understood how insensitive my remarks were, considering the little time that had passed since his accident and surgery. He simply didn't feel lucky quite yet.

In the silence of my place of spiritual rest, I became much more acutely aware of the wider dimensions of my family situation. For me, this awareness draws me even closer to my Creator who leads me to ways of becoming more compassionate and caring in my dealings with others.

Listen some more.

Listen. Reflecting on the faces of my children helped me see them in a different light. I also need to replay the sounds of my day during prayer. This form of interior listening helps me understand what they really need from me. One day, during prayer, I thought about a conversation I had with a woman in my community. She and I both tried out for the lead in our town's spring musical production.

She got the lead, and I had a small part in the chorus. One day, during rehearsal, when she was having an especially bad time with her lines, she walked over to me and made some remark about how things would have gone if I had gotten her part.

For some reason, I put the wrong connotation on her words. Feeling hurt, I went home from rehearsal that night trying to figure out what she meant by her remarks to me. Was she trying to rub my nose in the fact that she won the part and I didn't?

The next morning, I considered her words again in the silence of my prayer time. I became more conscious of my own hardness of heart and my prejudice toward others. I understood that what she really was saying was, "I'm not sure I was the right choice for this part. You seem to be so confident on stage. Perhaps you could have done a better job."

Instead of saying nothing and walking away hurt, I should have reassured her that she was doing a wonderful job (which she was). By taking the time to reconsider her words during my prayer time, I was able to amend my selfish ways the next time I saw her. At the first opportunity that presented itself, I genuinely complimented her on her character interpretation of a certain scene.

She looked at me with appreciation and said, "I respect you and value your feedback."

Keeping in touch. During silent time, review your relationships with those both at home, on the job, and in the community. When I thought about my relationship with the woman from my theater group, I was able to think through how I became out of touch with her. In reflection, I was able to come up with a creative way to reconcile.

Do this for yourself and others, too. Then when you go back home or into the world, you will know what appropriate gesture will offer encouragement and support to those you serve.

CAN YOU COME OUT AND PLAY?

All work and no play makes Jill a dull girl. We haven't said much thus far about goofing off, but if you aren't having fun being a mom, a wife, and a worker bee in the world, isn't it time for another makeover?

Every woman I interviewed for this book eventually learned how to play again.

Naomi Rhode loves to play with her daughters. "We are always finding excuses to run off and play together. We've given our playtime a sense of legitimacy by calling one of our fun excursions the annual MD (medical-dental or mother-daughter) Retreat.

> **Review your relationships in the silence of your prayer.**

Once a year, Naomi and her daughters go off to places such as London; Vail, Colorado; Sedona, Arizona; or Seattle.

"Each year I buy my daughters something special that relates to our heritage. One year I had heritage coats made out of laces that my mother had given me.

"Next year's retreat, I am doing a book of memories for each one of them. These retreats are very important to all three of us. We giggle, go to the movies, get massages, eat fudge, and do things we wouldn't get to do if the guys were with us.

"This year both of my daughters had newborn infants who were only a few weeks old. Both daughters were nursing mommies. So we took the babies and off we went to Sedona, Arizona, and holed up in a condo for a few days. It was absolutely wonderful."

I love playing with all my daughters, too. We are a bunch of dancing fools and disco freaks who love to go trash disco on Thursday night. My husband hates disco music, so he usually goes fishing or to a movie with the brothers. Last Halloween we marathon disco danced for six hours. Warning: If you are over fifty like I am, make sure your local chiropractor is within cracking distance.

Debbie Sarnowski says nothing beats getting out and playing with other moms on the block once a week.

"It keeps me going because every week, something funny and exciting happens. A few weeks ago, the girls took me bowling for my birthday. We ended up being on the national news. Here is what happened.

"First we went out to eat and then we went to our local bowling alley in Milwaukee. When we got there, a guy around twenty-one years old was bowling without a shirt on. We were kind of embarrassed, so we went up to the guy at the front desk and asked him why the kid didn't have a shirt on. He pointed to a sign over the counter that read: Bowl Naked and Bowl Free.

"The sign was supposed to be a joke. Evidently, they put it up one day when the air conditioning went on the fritz. So we go back to our lane, and the kid is now down to just wearing his red boxer shorts.

"I am really getting mad. I go back to the manager and complain while my girlfriends sit there. By the time I get back with the manager, the guy is stark naked, and he is bowling up a storm.

"We started screaming and covering our eyes. The manager is screaming at him to get dressed. But he was getting so obnoxious that we went and got the cops. Anyhow, the cops arrested him, and we all had to go to the police line and identify him. He was laughing and waving at us through the reverse glass."

A few mornings later, Debbie was driving to work and listening to her car radio. The radio talk show host said, "If anyone saw the naked bowler, please call in. Better yet, if you are one of the church ladies, call in."

Debbie found out that Jay Leno picked up the naked bowler story in her local newspaper. For some reason, he told the story on TV about the "church ladies in their nineties who were egging this guy on to take off his clothes. But we are all moms in our thirties, and it had been awhile since we had been to church."

Debbie said, "My birthday party with the naked bowler has kept us going for months."

Sometimes all we need is a little time to go out and play. But please, mothers, keep your clothes on.

INVENTORY OF STRENGTHS

At the end of Chapter 1, I talked about the importance of finding ways to continually reenter an attitude-of-gratitude state of mind. Possessing that attitude ensures your makeover.

Celebrate your life and the lives of those around you.

Sometimes all it takes to regain such a state of bliss is to participate in activities or create experiences that accentuate our strengths and assets as human beings. Here is an Inventory of Strengths Sheet to help you get started. Follow the instructions and start celebrating who you are by doing what you love the next time the opportunity presents itself.

INVENTORY OF STRENGTHS

Instructions: The following is a list of strengths and assets people may possess. Take a separate piece of paper and record all of the strengths on this sheet you believe you have. That includes things listed you have enjoyed in the past.

SPORTS AND OUTDOOR ACTIVITIES: Active participation in outdoor activities and organized sports, camping, hiking, etc. Regular exercise program.

HOBBIES AND CRAFTS: All hobbies, crafts, and related interests including any instruction or training in such crafts as weaving, pottery, and jewelry making. Any other interest to which you give time.

EXPRESSIVE ARTS: Any type of dancing. Any form of writing (stories, essays, poetry). Sketching, painting, sculpture, modeling with clay. Ability to improvise music or play a musical instrument, definite rhythmic ability, and so forth.

HEALTH: Good health represents a strength. List any measures for maintaining or improving your health, including seeking adequate medical treatment when needed, yearly medical checkups, and any other means designed for this purpose.

EDUCATION, TRAINING, AND RELATED AREAS: All education beyond grade school, including high school, college, advanced study, specialty schools, on-the-job training, seminars, special courses you have taken, self-education, study, and organized reading. Any high grades, any scholastic and related honors.

WORK, VOCATION, JOB, OR POSITION: Include here years of experience in a particular line of work (sales, management) as well as having successfully held different positions or received awards. Owning or managing your own firm. Job satisfaction including enjoying your work, good relations with coworkers, feelings of satisfaction with customers and staff.

SPECIAL APTITUDES OR RESOURCES: Having hunches or making guesses that usually turn out right. Following through on these hunches. Having a green thumb. Mechanical ability. Sales ability. Mathematical ability. Skill with hands in constructing and repairing things.

STRENGTHS THROUGH FAMILY AND OTHERS: Having a spouse who gives love, affection, understanding, and is interested in things you are doing and gives support. Relationships with children or parents that are sources of satisfaction or strength. Close relationship with other relatives and close friends as a source of strength.

INTELLECTUAL STRENGTHS: Applying reasoning ability to problem solving. Intellectual curiosity. Thinking out ideas and expressing them verbally or in writing. Being able to accept new ideas. Doing original or creative thinking. Having the ability to learn and enjoy learning.

AESTHETIC STRENGTHS: Recognizing and enjoying beauty in nature, the arts, or people and as expressed through the personality of people. Using aesthetic sense to enhance home and physical environment.

ORGANIZATIONAL STRENGTHS: Developing and planning sensible, short-range goals. Carrying out orders as well as giving them. Experience in organizing enterprises; projects; clubs; social, political, or other organizations. Leadership positions in key voluntary and fundraising projects.

IMAGINATIVE AND CREATIVE STRENGTHS: Using creativity and imagination for new and different ideas in relation to home, family, or vocation. Working on developing and extending your imaginative and creative abilities.

RELATIONSHIP STRENGTHS: Ability to meet people easily, make them feel comfortable. Ability to talk freely to strangers. Good relations with neighbors. Treating people with consideration, politeness, and respect. Being aware of the needs and feelings of others. Being able to really listen to what others have to say. Helping others to be aware of their strengths and abilities as well as their shortcomings or problems. Relating to people as individuals regardless of so-called barriers. Giving people the feeling that you understand them.

SPIRITUAL STRENGTHS: Feeling close to God, a supreme force, or nature. Living what you believe. Being humble. Recognizing the dignity and brotherhood of all men.

EMOTIONAL STRENGTHS: Ability to give as well as to receive affection and love. Being able to feel a wide range of emotions. Being able to do or express things on the spur of the moment. The ability to put yourself in the other person's shoes, to feel what he or she feels. Understanding the role of your feelings and emotions in everyday living.

OTHER STRENGTHS: Making the best of your appearance by means of good grooming and a discriminating choice of clothes.

HUMOR: As a source of strength—being able to laugh at yourself and to take kidding at your own expense.

ADVENTURE: Trying new ways of doing things, pioneering, exploring new horizons.

This inventory is being passed down to you from a very special lady. Remember the sad story in the first chapter about my best friend? After her funeral, her husband gave me some of her favorite books. Inside, between one of the pages, was a folded piece of paper. I unfolded it and discovered the Inventory of Strengths Sheet.

It is my hope and prayer that you will use this inventory as a guide to find many reasons to celebrate your existence.

Notes

Chapter One

9–10 Gallagher, Maggie. "Shame May Be Good, But Guilt Is Better." *USA Today*, March 13, 1997, p. 15A.

12–13 Canfield and Hansen's *Chicken Soup for the Soul*.

Chapter Two

29 Schmit, Julie. "Reality Bites Workers in Form of Kids, Spouses and Life." *USA Today*, April 22, 1997, p. B1.

40 Wilde, Anna D. "Its a New Generation of Business Travelers." *The New York Times*, November 12, 1995, p. F1.

42 Kaplan, Lisa Faye. "Spock Reflects on His Baby Revolution." *USA Today*, October 22, 1996, p. 4D.

46–47 DeParle, Jason. "Sheila Burke is the Militant Feminist Commie Peacenik Who's Telling Bob Dole What to Think." *The New York Times Magazine*, November 12, 1995, p. 36.

Chapter Three

53 Hancock, LynNell. "Breaking Point." *Newsweek*, March 6, 1995, p. 60.

54 Silverstein, Olga. "Voices in the Fatherhood Debate." *Los Angeles Times*, March 1, 1994, p. E4.

55 Wallerstein, Judith. "What Do Children Really Need?" *Los Angeles Times*, March 16, 1995, p. E12.

69–70 Wong, Jan. "When Women Earn the Bread." *The Globe and the Mail*, February 17, 1996, p. A8.

Chapter Four

78 Chawla, Navin. *Mother Teresa: The Authorized Biography*, Rockport, Mass.: p. xxiv. 1996 USA publication, Element Books, Inc. PO Box 830, Rockport, MA 01966.

82–86 "How to Begin Your Exercise Program." Courtesy of IDEA: The Health & Fitness Source, San Diego, CA (619-535-8979).

93 "What Do Children Really Need?" *Los Angeles Times*, March 16, 1995. David Royko, psychologist for Family Counseling Services in Cook County, IL., p. E1.

94 Father Anthony DeMello. *Wake Up and Live* audiotapes. The Institute of Jesuit Sources, 3700 W. Pine Blvd., St. Louis, MO 63108.

96 Bragg, Ginna. *A Simple Celebration*. Harmony Books, 1997. Great vegetarian cookbook and Deepak Chopra's chef. A great read!

85 "What Do Children Really Need?" *Los Angeles Times*.

Chapter Five

111 Johnson, Dirk. "Uncertain Future on Their Own Awaits." *The New York Times*, March 16, 1997, p. 1.

115 Munk, Nina. "The Best Man for Your Job Is Your Wife." *Forbes*, November 20, 1995, p. 152.

136 Goodman, Ellen. "The Rigged Tax Laws Making the Lives of Working Moms Difficult." *The Idaho Statesman*, April 15, 1997, p. 7A.

Chapter Six

153 Mandino, Og. *The Spellbinder's Gift*. 1995, Fawcett Crest, NY.

164–165 Ellas, Marilyn. "A Woman's Work Is Key to Her Well-being." *USA Today*, August 20, 1996, p. 6D.

Chapter Seven

173–175 Catherine Marshall. *Beyond Ourselves*. 1961, McGraw-Hill, Spire. Books paperback. By permission of McGraw-Hill. Chapter 12, "Ego-Slaying," pp. 189–194.

For your next Seminar or Convention invite Danielle Kennedy to speak. Contact:

Danielle Kennedy Productions
P.O. Box 1395
Sun Valley ID 83353
208-726-8375 • Fax: 208-726-9631 • 800-848-8070
email: daniellekennedy@svidaho.net
Internet: http://www.daniellekennedy.com

SEVEN FIGURE SELLING

Proven Secrets to Success from Top Sales Professionals

DANIELLE KENNEDY

Sales professionals, entrepreneurs, and small business owners alike will learn sales strategies and gain the mindset that can truly lead to surpassing $1,000,000 sales and business goals! Tactical strategies and candid stories from legendary sales professionals— like Jenny Craig, Founder and President of Jenny Craig International; Helen Gurley Brown, Editor of Cosmopolitan; Judi Sheppard Missett, Founder of Jazzercise International; Fred Segal, Owner of Fred Segal Stores; and many more—offer new insight into the "out-of-the-box" thinking that set these businesses leaps and bounds ahead of the rest.

0-324-18751-3 ©2003

Danielle Kennedy, a sales legend in her own right, pulls the "*best of the best*" success strategies and the characteristics of a business winner into one dynamic resource providing the tools needed to launch a sales career or business to the next level of higher profits. Learn about:

- Using Imagination as a Powerful Business Force
- The Rewards of the Payback Philosophy
- Predicting Patterns of Buying Behavior
- Creating Excitement and Building Trust
- Renewing Your Energy for Unparalleled Performance
- How to Listen Like a Lover

Order your copy today!
http://www.thomsonlearning.com/catalogs/
1-800-354-9706, option 4

ISBN 0-324-18751-3

HOW TO LIST & SELL REAL ESTATE

Executing New Basics for Higher Profits

DANIELLE KENNEDY & WARREN JAMISON

How to List & Sell Real Estate

EXECUTING NEW BASICS FOR HIGHER PROFITS

Danielle Kennedy
with Warren Jamison

0-324-18776-9 ©2003

This best-selling real estate book delivers the proven formula for a fast-track career and higher profits. Let Kennedy—one of real estate's most highly regarded professionals—be your mentor as a new or seasoned agent. Jump-start your career and become a 100 percent referral agent by returning to timeless trade secrets for building life-long customers and gaining market share. Discover why technology will not replace the agent's value but, instead, increase the demand for personalized selling!

The newest edition includes:
- New and expanded methods to convert a sales prospect and build loyalty.
- The 21-Day Breakaway Schedule (a beginner's guide to fast results) with Internet strategies.
- How to capture the "For Sale By Owner" business electronically.
- eCommunication secrets and "cell phonology" for faster follow-up and increased prospects.
- No More Sales Slumps—the open house campaign that produces immediate results!
- Why collaboration is the best way to list and sell in all markets.
- **NOW on CD-ROM**—Danielle's **Money-Making Forms** in interactive Excel® files.

Order your copy today!
http://www.thomsonlearning.com/catalogs/
1-800-354-9706, option 4

ISBN 0-324-18776-9